# The
# Magical World of
# OWEN
# BARFIELD

## Gareth Knight

Sun Chalice

Published by

Sun Chalice Books

PO Box 5355, Oceanside. CA 92052   USA

sunchalice@earthlink.com

Library of Congress Control Number:  **2002102306**

ISBN 1-928754-10-4

*Cover and book design by Nicholas Whitehead*

# TABLE OF CONTENTS

# I

# THE WISEST AND THE BEST OF TEACHERS

"To Owen Barfield, wisest and best of my unofficial teachers"

This is the dedication to be found in *The Allegory of Love,* the book that established the academic reputation of C.S.Lewis; and according to Humphrey Carpenter, the biographer of that group of Oxford friends who became known as the Inklings, Lewis "regarded Barfield as in every way an intellectual equal and in some respects superior to himself."

Unlike Lewis, Barfield did not pursue an academic career, although in later life, after retirement from the legal profession, he did enjoy a long period as a visiting professor at a number of American universities. This went on almost until his death at the age of 98. In his native land, however, he remained largely "a prophet without honour." Whether this was due to a professional closing of ranks to one perceived to be an academic outsider is a matter of conjecture. Certainly Sir Herbert Read felt this to be the case, and was moved to write to *The Listener* (an intellectual review published by the British Broadcasting Corporation) "it is not quite true to say that non-academic critics of literature do not exist today – it is merely that academic critics ignore them. I am not alone in thinking that a country solicitor such as Mr Owen Barfield is superior to all the academic critics mentioned …. This was also the opinion of that distinguished editor, publisher, and non-academic critic, the late T.S.Eliot."

Barfield and Lewis met as undergraduates at Oxford in 1919, after army service. Barfield had served in the signals section of the Royal Engineers from 1917 after winning a scholarship in classics to Wadham College, Oxford. He became very interested in English literature while he was in the army and when he finally arrived at Oxford he managed to switch his scholarship to a course in English literature in which he gained a first class honours degree. The dissertation that Barfield wrote for his Bachelor of Literature degree in 1922 achieved the dignity of a published book in 1928 as *Poetic Diction*.

C.S.Lewis cited it as an authority in his own academic work, *The Allegory of Love*. Nor was he alone in his appreciation of Barfield's book, for in the words of Professor G.B.Tennyson: "No book by Owen Barfield is more deserving of serious attention from students of literature and thought than *Poetic Diction*. This extraordinary study stands virtually alone in focusing on the mysterious area in poetry between word and meaning." It dealt in effect with the magical roots of language, and its consequent power, particularly in heightened and inspired or "poetic" form.

Barfield also showed early promise with his book *History in English Words*, in 1926, which was almost equally highly regarded, attracting in its later editions a foreword by W.H.Auden, who regarded it as "a privilege to be allowed to recommend a book which is not only a joy to read but also of great moral value as a weapon in the unending battle between civilisation and barbarism."

In terms of published work therefore, he was somewhat in advance of his more famous friend C.S.Lewis. Both of them came under the influence of J.R.R.Tolkien, who was appointed to a professorial chair at Oxford in 1922. It was a major concern of Barfield, that was not lost upon a philologist such as Tolkien, that the use of language is an intimate and revealing expression of the state of consciousness of any race, nation or society, and its evolution.

In 1922 Barfield became a member of the Anthroposophical Society, founded by Rudolf Steiner, and thus became a channel for esoteric ideas that he hammered out at length in long conversations with Lewis on walking weekends and holidays. The substance of these conversations was no doubt the grist to the mill that sustained a life-long friendship between the two and an ongoing debate that they came to refer to as "the Great War". They undoubtedly had a certain influence each upon the other, part of which is discernible in Lewis's fiction and conversely perhaps Barfield's later affiliation to the Church of England in 1945. However, he never abandoned his anthroposophical beliefs, even if Lewis thought some of them of doubtful compatibility with Christian orthodoxy. The original edition of *Poetic Diction* was dedicated "To C.S.Lewis – opposition is true friendship" – and in the preface to the third edition, written twenty-four years later, that dedication is renewed, "in celebration of nearly half a lifetime's priceless friendship."

Barfield also tried his hand at children's fiction and his story *The Silver Trumpet* was published in 1925 and attained reasonable sales. However, financial pressures did not allow Barfield to try to make a living from his pen and so he took up the practice of law, at which he spent most of his working life.

Apart from a collection of occasional articles and lectures published in 1944 as *Romanticism Comes of Age*, he published no more books until the semi-autobiographical *This Ever Diverse Pair* in 1950 a few years before his retirement. His retirement, when it came, turned out to be a very fruitful period with a number of thought provoking works. The first of them was a philosophical work analysing the faculties of perception, *Saving the Appearances,* in 1957, followed by two in the form of Socratic dialogues or symposia, *Worlds Apart* and *Unancestral Voice* in 1963 and 1965.  He then produced a major work on romantic philosophy, *What Coleridge Thought,* in 1972. During this period he was "discovered" and encouraged by American academe and, largely as a result of visiting lectureships, books of collected essays and talks appeared: *Speaker's Meaning* (1967), *The Rediscovery of Meaning* (1977) and *History, Guilt and Habit* (1979). In later life he also wrote a play, *Orpheus,* encouraged by Lewis, that enshrined many of his philosophical ideas.

Barfield's fundamental opinions changed little over the years, save in natural development and increasing cogency of expression. Three broad themes run through them all:

i) the importance of the imagination;
ii) the evolution of human consciousness;
iii) how this evolution is revealed in the changing meanings of words.

# II

## THE IMPORTANCE OF THE IMAGINATION

Owen Barfield records in his introduction to *Romanticism Comes of Age* that he was brought up as an agnostic but that the intellectual vacuum created by his scepticism was broken at about the age of twenty-one by an increasing intensity in the way that he experienced lyric poetry. This was not so much a reaction to whole poems but more to the way certain word combinations worked on his mind.

"It seemed there was some magic in it;" he writes, "and a magic which not only gave me pleasure but also reacted on and expanded the meanings of the individual words concerned." Furthermore, he found that this heightened experience of the poetic use of words spilled over into his appreciation of the outer world, of nature, art, history and human relationships, throwing up significances he otherwise would not have realised.

He records two fundamental conclusions from this direct experience:

i) poetic or imaginative use of words enhances their meanings;

ii) those enhanced meanings may reveal hitherto unapprehended parts of aspects of reality. He goes on to emphasise this second point by saying, "I found I knew (there was no other word for it) things about them which I had not known before."

It was the pursuit and investigation of this phenomenon that led to his writing *Poetic Diction* and *History in English Words*.

The ground base of these studies was the work of the English Romantic poets, particularly Wordsworth and Coleridge, underpinned by Shakespeare, and a good deal of general philosophy, particularly that which borders on psychology, including the Greek of the later Platonic Dialogues and relevant parts of Aristotle, such as his work on the soul, *De Anima*.

During this period, however, Romanticism in general was under an intellectual cloud, partly through disillusionment following the First World War, and partly through hopes of a socialist panacea. However, Barfield felt himself engaged in a longer term battle. One that was not simply confined to the twentieth century but one in which Coleridge and the Romantic poets had also been engaged.

This was the fight against materialist reductionism, that had become increasingly part and parcel of the popular scientific outlook since the seventeenth century. He saw all this in a yet larger perspective in terms of the history of human consciousness, a perspective that he gained from the study of Rudolf Steiner's works. Most of Barfield's books are deeply reasoned and observed justifications for this belief.

Moreover, he saw this line of study as no mere academic dalliance with ancient usage, but as of vital importance to bringing about the next stage in the evolution of human consciousness, in which modern man is in desperate need of help and guidance, as the political and economic state of the world makes evident.

# III

## THE EVOLUTION OF HUMAN CONSCIOUSNESS

Barfield traces the evolution of human consciousness from a state of "involvement" in the phenomena of the world at large, and in this there is a parallel with the evolution of consciousness in the maturing individual, from infancy to adulthood.

Early man, like the modern infant, did not experience the world as the mature modern adult does – as an individual, standing alone, in an external universe which he is disengaged from, even to the point of apparent alienation. Early man, like the infant, participated intimately in the world of nature, which was like a mother's love. There was not the differentiation from the environment that is taken for granted nowadays.

This is particularly evident in the power of the totem animal. A tribe so identifies with a bird or beast that the species is indistinguishable from the tribe itself and from individuals who make up the tribe. Individuals, although bodily separate, are more mutually participative. The feelings, the assumptions, the customs of the group, have an overpowering influence on the individual psyche. This is akin to the psychology of the crowd, be it concernt audience, football club, or lynch mob. A modern crowd is a relatively transient entity but a primitive tribe more permanent. Certain anthropologists have coined the term "participation mystique" to describe this mode of consciousness. This replaced the earlier naïve theories that primitive peoples think in the same way that we do, speculate about the nature of natural phenomena in an intellectual fashion, and because they are more stupid, get it wrong! Thus implying that mythological stories about gods and spirits in the storm and rain was the best they could do in the scientific discipline of meteorology!

These earlier anthropological theories made the elementary blunder of assuming that primitive man's mode of mentation was the same as our own. It is Barfield's point that early man did not think "about" the nature of an external world as we do. He was more identified with it, so that it is doubtful if he would have been able to conceive what we mean by such a term as "external world" let alone set about "explaining" it. Only gradually did a sense of individuality, a separated ego, begin to develop.

And with this development comes the ability to distinguish the self from the environment, along with which comes the ability to record experience. That is, at this stage, we have the origin of language, at first spoken, and much, much later, written. It is easy to overlook the important implications of the formation of language. It is the faculty above all that distinguishes men from the beasts. It is the animal world that would seem to be almost totally identified with its environment.

As soon as man started to individualise from animal-man he could begin to identify discrete objects and make words to represent them. This is the stage represented in the Bible where Adam "names" all the creatures. Naming external objects is an identifiable stage in the process of individuation, and by it man begins to identify himself. Much the same occurs in the development of the child, when dawning self-consciousness goes hand in hand with the development of language. In course of time words begin to be written, and from this we are better able, with our modern analytical consciousness, to trace evidence of the continuing evolution of consciousness during recorded historical time.

This includes the recording of myth and legend which the earliest writings record as actual events of the past. Here we must guard against assuming that the minds of the time, even at this comparatively late stage, were as ours are today. The myths and legends and heroic sagas are not necessarily high-flown fancies embroidering prosaic fact, but may be actual records of what those of the time experienced.

This puts new light on the stories of the gods. We may choose, if we will, to explain away those ancient encounters as exaggerations of old tales, misunderstandings of natural phenomena, or psychological projections, but these are merely our contemporary interpretations of a mode of reality to which we deny existence and fail to understand. We ought to consider the possibility that the events of the Iliad, of the Odyssey, and all great tales of the pantheons of ancient gods and heroes are accurate records of real experience. The various heroes, Hector, Achilles, and the rest, saw the presence and heard the instruction of Pallas Athene, Hera, Aphrodite, Ares, Zeus, in the conduct of the Trojan war. The Erinyes were very real furies to Orestes; Dionysus a very real being to the Maenads and King Pentheus. We have no reason to doubt the veracity of these accounts other than our own latter day scepticism and disbelief that poses as common sense. It is our natural assumption, based upon our different type of consciousness, that all these tales are simply "made up" by the poet just as a modern writer of fiction "makes up" a story.

Barfield, having drawn attention to this, was not advocating that we try to return to this earlier mode of consciousness. This would be an error that is found in regressive mediumship or "solar plexus" psychism. However, he believed that as a first step we should recognise the validity, in their own time, of these ancient forms of perception. Then, if we can realise that there is a *process* in the unfolding of human consciousness, we may be able to find for ourselves a way of release from the prison house of modern reductionist assumptions, and a way forward to a higher form of consciousness that is now striving to be born.

This is the basis of Barfield's investigation of the use of language, and he aimed to show evidence of this evolution of consciousness by the change of meaning in particular words. In *Poetic Diction* he advocated that a history of language be written, not from the logician's point of view but from the insights of the poet. He even outlined the course that such a vast work might be expected to follow.

# IV

## LANGUAGE AND THE EVOLUTION OF CONSCIOUSNESS

In the early period of written record that are the great sagas of the Vedas in India, the *Iliad* and the *Odyssey* in Greece, where "Nature is alive in the thinking of man", the gods are the springs of action and spiritual beings walk the Earth. It is because they are a direct record of a wider experience that they bring a sense of sublimity and have the vitality to have made their appeal through the ages. They have the power of childhood memories, images of immensities that can be recalled in later life by the adult, and give spiritual insight to forgotten realities that may still abide. Wordsworth tried to exemplify this in *The Prelude*. These old stories are no arbitrary fancies but the direct record of conscious experience in the childhood of the human race. However, with the passage of time, and the development of the individualised ego there comes a corresponding loss of vividness of these modes of experience. We come, in the time of Plato, to a stage where these forces and beings are not direct personal experiences but philosophical abstractions, or Ideas. We must guard against the error of assuming that such Ideas were as cerebral and abstract to Plato as the modern experience of ideas is to us. They were realised as mighty forces behind the natural world; were regarded as more permanent than the natural world; and indeed as being the root causes of the natural world. They are close to being angelic beings, sub-creators, or what in Tolkien's world are called the Valar.

At the same time the role of the poet had been changing. From being the mouthpiece of the gods overtaken by a divine frenzy or inspiration, the poet begins to take a greater measure of personal responsibility for "his" creative work. Even so, for a long time, it was the practice to invoke the Muses at the commencement of any major poetic effort of creation. We see it in Spenser and also in Milton, and it is by no means entirely an empty convention even in the modern age. The early Greek dramatists met in competition, albeit at religious festivals, and with their material related to matters of the heroes and the gods. And we can trace an increasingly individualistic approach from the earlier hieratic formalities of Aeschylus, to the more flexible, individual, idiosyncratic approach of Euripides. Thus began the secularisation of the theatre. Even so, the plays were designed to bring about a religious experience, a catharsis induced by pity and horror, and then relieved by comedy. The impact of poetry and drama would have been much greater in those days. We should remember that it was the *spoken* word that was the medium of communication, with all its incantatory power. The historian Macaulay makes this point:

> Men will talk about the old poets, and comment on them, and to a certain degree enjoy them. But they will scarcely be able to conceive the effect which poetry produced on their ruder ancestors, the agony, the ecstasy, the plenitude of belief.

And he exemplifies this with the humane assumption, drawn from contemporary annals, "The Mohawk hardly feels the scalping knife when he shouts his death song." If this be true it would appear to give an advantage to the more primitive over the more civilised in the course of battle, sophistication of weaponry being equal! Gibbon records the use of bards by the Teutons to stir them in time of war. Indeed we have the Celtic tradition of the bards being formidable aids to warfare on the battlefield, their satires being sufficiently powerful to raise blisters on the faces of their enemies! This is certainly a poetic (or magical) power of the human voice that is scarcely available to moderns, because of the development of the ego. We are more cut off, but at the same time more protected, from the magical world. Even so, public opinion can be an important factor in our behaviour.

Barfield saw this period of gradual emergence of the individual consciousness from the group as marked by the spread of the written word. The invention of the printing press would thus mark a major external change that signified the burgeoning internal one. There was then a phase change, so to speak, at the end of the sixteenth century, with the individual perception breaking free from the vestiges of participation mystique. This coincides with the beginnings of the scientific method which, at the beginning of the seventeenth century, is largely associated with the programme of ideas advanced by Francis Bacon. We must however distinguish between the history of ideas and the history of consciousness. It is the emergence of human consciousness from one stage of growth to another that is the underlying cause of the influx of new ideas, including the invention of the necessary technology. A superficial examination of the history of ideas might otherwise lead one to assume that human beings were too stupid before the seventeenth century to apply their minds to science and technology, or that prior to then all scientific knowledge had been repressed by the vested interests of religious dogma.

Why then did not the ancient civilisations, all capable of formidable feats of structural engineering, not develop the scientific method? They were certainly bright enough to have done so. But it would seem that it just did not occur to them to apply a mechanistic, reductionist approach to the world about them. Was it because they were so aware of a vibrant multi-dimensional universe of which they were all a part that such an approach would appear ridiculous? This vibrant multi-dimensional world is no longer available to man because his consciousness has become individualised to a greater degree. He is a prisoner in solitary confinement within his own cranium. Barfield considered this to be, not an unmitigated disaster, but a necessary stage in the evolution of consciousness. In order to establish the ego, and its inalienable spiritual rights, man needs to feel alone. Only in this way, by going through the phase of feeling an insignificant speck in a vast and alien universe, can he take upon himself the full responsibility of his destiny.

Having experienced to the full the implications of being a spiritual monad, the way forward is to reopen consciousness to the wider perspective that has been temporarily lost. This does not mean a reversion to the old participation mystique, which would be a regression into superstition and cosmic childhood, but an opening of individual conscious responsibility to the greater whole. This implies the growing awareness that the planet which man inhabits, and of which he is steward and guardian, is a living organism, containing living organisms within all its parts, even the most seemingly inert, and part of a great hierarchy of living organisms that spans the stars. The immediate way forward has been shown, Barfield believed, by certain way-showers of the past two hundred years. Of particular note are the eighteenth century German poet-scientist Goethe, and the English Romantic poet-thinker Coleridge.

When we look for further evidence of a changing mode of consciousness and perception (the two are intimately interlinked) we need hardly go further than medieval painting. Why was there no perspective? Medieval art looks "quaint" to us because of the lack of this convention to which we have grown accustomed. Why did the medieval artist and his public feel no need for it? Perspective is a device that gives an impression of the world as it is viewed from a unique point in space. That is, through the eyes of a single beholder. From the eye holes in an individual head. Before this time, it would seem, reality could be very satisfactorily represented in two dimensions, with the size of the figures indicating their social or spiritual status, arguably more important than the mere physical distance in space from some arbitrary observer.

The spiritual was part and parcel of the everyday world. Angels might be given the convention of wings to indicate their heavenly origin and function but they were dressed in the ordinary fashions of the day. Similarly the vehicle which transported Elijah to heaven could be of the same type and design as a contemporary farm cart, without in any way seeming incongruous. Yet to many people nowadays it would seem ludicrous, even blasphemous, to see Elijah going to heaven in a motor car, or even a space ship, or to see angels dressed in contemporary city suits or sweat shirts and jeans.

And when we turn to philosophical writings of the medieval period we find it almost impossible to follow the train of thought. Scholastic philosophers had a fineness of perception, and an ability for intellectual analysis and definition that is at least the equal of modern minds. But even if we can follow the arguments, say, of Thomas Aquinas about "species and genus, form and matter, subject and accident" it is only with the greatest difficulty that we can effect that alteration of intellectual perspective to appreciate what he really meant.

# V

## WHAT COLERIDGE TAUGHT

The whole medieval world picture is described in some detail by C.S.Lewis in *The Discarded Image,* a study aid for students of English literature to help them get their minds back into the frame of consciousness that was implicit in medieval and early Renaissance life and thought. At a slightly more distant remove we might also cite Lewis' hilarious depiction of the Dark Age historical Merlin turning up in a suburban villa in modern times, to indicate the differences in the assumptions of each age.[†] The point is, that to all concerned, they are much more than just assumptions, they are a self-evident reality! Difference in perception is the key to much of this problem, and this is the reason for Barfield's emphasis on the significance of Coleridge's theory of the imagination.

According to Coleridge we input a great deal of our imagination into our perception of the world about us. A blind man newly given sight has to "learn" to see – to sort out the teeming mass of incoming sensations into a picture that makes sense. This is the function of what he called the Primary Imagination. It is a creative act, which we usually take for granted. Beyond this is the Secondary Imagination that sees deeper significances and connections and might be identified with poetic inspiration, although its intuitive insights are equally applicable to science, technological invention, or any other area of life.

Coleridge saw the human spirit expressing itself through certain faculties which can be listed out schematically:

[†] C.S.Lewis: *That Hideous Strength*

REASON

IMAGINATION

UNDERSTANDING

====================

UNDERSTANDING

FANCY

SENSE

Reason is the highest element of consciousness in the human being, and is far removed from the intellectual faculty, which is called the Understanding by Coleridge. For him, Reason is what might elsewhere be more commonly designated as the Spirit.

Understanding, or the power of ratiocination, that is present in humans and to a lesser degree in some animals, is divided by a bar to designate two modes of it. The lower mode is that which derives from sense experience – the ability of rats to find their way through a maze after a process of trial and error is a limited example of this. The higher mode, found only in human beings, so far as we can judge, is ratiocination irradiated by reason, intuitively aware of the higher realms of existence beyond the material.

Imagination and Fancy are principally pictorial modes of mind working. Fancy is again a form of simple association of images derived from sense experience and Pavlov's dogs salivating through the association of food and a ringing bell is a basic example, although the juxtaposition of images can also be random or inconsequential.

Imagination, on the other hand, is a fusing, transforming, transcending faculty that is creative in its powers of changing and refining ideas and images. It is a coordinating rather than a mere agglomerative power. In its Primary mode it allows us to make ordered sense out of a host of sensory perceptions and in its Secondary mode gives expression to works of art or other forms of creative ability, or the appreciation thereof.

Nature itself, that provides the sense impressions, Coleridge also divides in a similar way:

*NATURA NATURANS* – "naturing" or creative nature

*NATURA NATURATA* – "natured" or created nature

This is a complete antithesis of the materialist viewpoint that all consciousness evolved from matter. Rather it considers all matter to be projected creations by denizens of a world of archetypal ideas and spiritual wills.

We have, furthermore, been conditioned by modern scientism to regard reality as something beyond visible appearances. That is to say, for instance, that the colour, texture and hardness of the world about us are secondary "illusions" of a more fundamental reality behind them that consists of electro-magnetic forces discernible only through an electron microscope, and that only indirectly.

To Coleridge such an idea would have been utterly false, as he insisted that:

a) all reality is in fact immediate;

b) we create reality in polar relationship with others;

c) what we practice is what IS.

These may seem arbitrary axiomatic statements but they are no more so than the assumptions made by Descartes and that are followed by materialistic promulgators of modern scientism, who insist that the subjective is separate from the objective.

Cartesian dualism, ingrained by habit of thought over several centuries, has the appearance of being obvious and common sense. However, as William Blake observed, we need to cleanse the doors of perception; and the cleansing that has to be done is to get rid of the Cartesian assumptions that we took in at our mother's knee, and with which we have continued to be tacitly indoctrinated, without necessarily ever having heard of Descartes or reading his philosophy.

The human intellect, (the lower form of Understanding in Coleridge's schema), can only attempt to explain phenomena by recourse to another line of phenomena (atoms, molecules, force-fields, etc.). From these, various scientific theories may be spun, but these are but webs of fancy attempting to explain appearances. Although later scientific thinkers may smile with indulgence on earlier fancies, such as the theories of phlogiston, geocentrism, or the like, their own fancies, couched in terms of higher mathematics or computational data, are no nearer to fundamental reality. Owen Barfield drew particular attention to this in *Saving the Appearances*.

As far as Coleridge was concerned, the solution of phenomena can never be derived from phenomena. We have to grasp the fact that the underlying reality of things is not matter, or any equivalent inanimate base external to ourselves, but is an immediate and immaterial relationship. In other words, the principle of polarity lies at the foundation of the world.

This basic polarity lies firstly between the creator and the created; that is, between natura naturans and natura naturata; between human higher consciousness and lower consciousness; between an oversoul and individual members of a plant or animal species; all of which might be termed, for diagrammatic convenience, "vertical polarity".

Equally important however is "horizontal polarity" between

creators, and between their creations, which produces the worlds of perceived phenomena. In common psychological terms this is an act of imagination. Our imagination constructs the world that appears about us. The act of perception, which is instantaneous and unconscious in its workings, is an activity of what Coleridge called the Primary Imagination. Thus do we create ourselves, in conjunction with the related other, be it the face of the beloved, the man in the Clapham omnibus, or other forms of spiritual consciousness.

In the fully consciously evolved man these perceptions, or primary imaginative pictures of relationships with others, are presented for assimilation by the higher faculties. That is to say, the powers of Higher Understanding; the Secondary or Creative Imagination; and pure Spiritual Reason.

The lower powers of Sense, Fancy and Lower Understanding – good servants but bad masters – provide functions of perception, memory and logical deduction respectively – all of which can nowadays be reproduced to a certain degree in computing devices. Human nature in its fullness, however, is capable of rather more than can be contained on a silicon chip.

It is by Reason and Imagination that we achieve our fullness as human beings. The Understanding, with its powers of analysis based upon experience, is a necessary device whereby we realise our own detachment from a common group, as discrete and individual beings. However, it needs to give way to, or to be enlightened by, the Imagination and Reason, which allow us to realise a higher form of unity and attachment, or, in Charles Williams' felicitous expression "co-inherence".

The realisations of Imagination and Reason are not easily formulated and grasped by the Understanding, for being polar, they tend to be expressible only in terms of paradox, or in terms of symbolic truth as in parable or myth. We enter the realm of Ideas, in Plato's sense, of living archetypes: "the prophetic soul of the wide world dreaming on things to come." Plato's nous is very similar in conception to Coleridge's Reason.

Coleridge's Reason, then, is the substance of ultimate reality, the power that produces and sustains the natural world. It is also the source of all laws of nature. In another sense it is God, which raises profound theological as well as psychological, philosophical and scientific questions. In the human being Reason irradiates consciousness but may be present to Understanding in two different modes, for although present, it may not be realised as being present, and therefore will be "unconscious" as opposed to being self-consciously realised.

We can tabulate the various terms that can be given to either of these two modes of Reason manifesting in the human psyche:

| Positive Mode | Negative Mode |
|---|---|
| Conscious Self-Knowledge | Unconscious Self-Knowledge |
| Positive Reason | Negative Reason |
| Active Reason | Passive Reason |
| Reason Awake | Dreaming Reason |
| Reason Perceived | Reason Idealised |
| Understanding "above the line" | Understanding "below the line" |

In its negative mode, unrealised and unconscious, Reason simply gives individuality to man, (no mean achievement of course on the evolutionary scale).

In its positive mode, it gives the spiritual awakening of the individual, (which is a yet higher level of attainment in the evolution of consciousness).

From this it will be seen that the distinction between Reason and Understanding is crucial. The unenlightened man, be he however intellectually brilliant or knowledgeable, is one in whom the lower Understanding has completely swallowed Reason. If he persists in remaining so dominated he is as a dreamer refusing to be awakened – an intellectual corpse refusing the golden destiny of resurrection.

There is also a paradox in the identity and action of Reason. It bestows individuality yet at the same time can never be considered plural. It is, in its essence, one and indivisible. An analogy may help the understanding of this paradox. We might consider all human individuals to be like burning candles – yet the light that individually they maintain is one indivisible principle that can be passed from one to another without diminishing itself.

Thus as well as the two modes of Reason that we have tabulated above, there are also two aspects of Reason – its individuality; and its universality (or super-individuality).

Reason bestows individuality to what would otherwise be a group-soul dominated animal psyche, by giving the faculty of abstraction, of generalising, of consequent detachment from sense phenomena and the ability to sort and categorise them in terms of universals. That is, to compare – which gives rise to logic – the ability to see whether any two conceptions in the mind are, or are not, in contradiction to each other. This faculty also implies a sense of detachment – of oneself as an autonomous unit, as subject, as object, in distinction from the environment.

However, this exercise of the passive or negative mode of Reason, which gives awareness of the aspect of individuality, is but a prison house if it becomes wholly concerned with the logic of difference in the realm of natura naturata, or created nature.

The paradox is brought about by a fundamental quality of

Reason, which is behind all manifested phenomena of which consciousness can become aware. This quality is the principle of Polarity.

We may now perhaps begin to comprehend why Imagination, in Coleridge's schema, is placed between Reason and Understanding. Linked to Understanding by the Imagination, Reason may make itself known to the human psyche. When it fails to do so then a lower condition prevails, in which Reason is swallowed up by the lower Understanding. Then the negative reasoning of logic dominates any attempted understanding of natura naturata – created nature – through the play of fancy spun into various theories, hypotheses and mental bric-a-brac of the unenlightened mind. This applies even to so-called religious sectors of life when an intellectually dogmatic and spiritually dry theology prevails over direct mystical consciousness or prophetic intuition.

The language of the Imagination is not the categorising limitations of logical classification, which of course does have its legitimacy at its own level and context, but in the enlarging dimensions of symbol and myth. The obsession with logical classification is one of the characteristics of Aunt Gamboy in Barfield's fairy tale *The Silver Trumpet,* a tale which in its symbolic wholeness is an example of the wider use of the Imagination.

Coleridge liked to present the nature of Reason by recourse to the myth of Prometheus, likening it to the fire that he brought from heaven to the lower world of men. And in a lecture of 1825 to the Royal Society of Literature he listed its characteristics as follows:

a)it was super-added, or infused, and no mere evolution from an animal basis;

b)it was "stolen from heaven" to mark its difference in kind from the qualities common to man and the higher animals;

c)its source in "heaven" marks its superiority as well as essential diversity;

d)it is a "spark", to mark that it is subject to no modifying reaction from that upon which it acts. It suffers no change from the inferior, but multiplies itself by conversion, without being alloyed by or amalgamated with that which it enobles, empowers and transforms;

e)it was stolen by a "god", and one of the dynasty before Jove, because Jove was the binder of reluctant powers, the coercer and entrancer of free spirits into the fetters of shape, mass and passive mobility. At the same time Prometheus was a god of the same race and essence as Jove, and linked in earlier days in closest and friendliest intimacy with him, to mark the pre-existence, in order of thought, of the nous, as spiritual, to the later products of the "coagulations of spirit" (to use Leibnitz' terms) and the objects of sense.

In other words, the spark of Reason, deriving from a god anterior to the Jovian dynasty, (that is, to the submersion of spirits into material forms), marks it as timeless, or eternal; superior to and different from all things that subsist in space and time. It is that which distinguishes man from the animal kingdom.

Coleridge sums up his interpretation of the Prometheus myth as the definition of Idea and Law – two concepts that are fundamental to the expression of Reason. The qualities of Reason simply ARE, and have to be accepted as facts of existence, in common with most existential realities – birth, death, growth, etc. That is its manifestation as Law.

In terms of Ideas of Reason we have to turn to poetic inspiration. Many poets say that when it comes to poetic composition of the highest order, then a brooding sense of presence is felt, and the poem "happens" to the poet, who with luck, skill and application, may be able to express it and write it down. Rather than the poet having an idea, it is a question of the Idea possessing the poet.

This is the mechanics not only of poetic inspiration but of inspiration in any of the arts or other endeavours of creative thought in man – Leonardo da Vinci, for example, was capable of expressing Ideas in scientific and technological as well as artistic and religious terms.

Coleridge compares the apprehension of an Idea of Reason with the experience of listening to music. One is at the same time constructing and being constructed by it. Similarly, reflection upon metaphysical ideas, such as the concept of a perfect circle in geometry, will develop a capacity for "inward beholding", or a means of access to the Ideas of Reason.

There is a similar principle at work in relation to man and God. God is in man and man is in God. God is therefore also in human society and human society in God. This is another way of looking at Reason, for Coleridge in his lecture on Prometheus states quite explicitly that "God is Reason".

For this reason Coleridge directed his readers to study the Bible, wherein a unified reality of God, Man, Nature and Society is apparent. To the lower understanding the events recorded therein may seem but annals of history, myth or legend to be intellectually assessed and evaluated as to their "objective" truth. However, looking at the text with the higher Understanding irradiated by Reason, a higher truth emerges, whereby the events recorded are seen as mutually illuminating realities and symbols. The act of perceiving this is an act of faith, that strengthens and perpetuates itself by its own activity.

Belief is a matter of rational judgement based upon evidence. Faith is an act of will; an act of fidelity to our own spiritual being.

Coleridge was convinced that if we approach the Bible with our Understanding irradiated by Reason then we will apprehend its wisdom as well as its history. He even urged his readers to an especial study of the Old Testament as teaching the elements of political science in the same sense as we refer to Euclid for the elements of the science of geometry!

When we reject the light of Reason we refute the ground of our own being, which ultimately is to deny our own humanity.

The true importance of Coleridge, and one which Barfield strove to demonstrate in his book *What Coleridge Thought* is that he points to a method whereby we can prove to ourselves, by reading in faith the annals of the sacred books, the unification of the natural, the divine and the social in the life expression that is the goal of our own individual evolution. Thereby we may approach closer to the true expression of the Divine will and love, and enter into harmonious relationships with other human beings and the whole concourse of nature. From Garden of Eden to New Jerusalem, with the Incarnation as the central point, the whole of life is there for whoever has "eyes to see and ears to hear".

# VI

## WHAT GOETHE SAW

In his psychology of perception and of true scientific method Coleridge insisted that we must accept the object as it is experienced, not try to explain it by recourse to a mathematical model, such as later was to become particularly evident in the popularised theories of atomic physics – patterns in an electromagnetic field behind the vibrant world of sense perception. In the realm of natural science however, it was the great German polymath Johann Wolfgang von Goethe (1749-1832) who best succeeded in setting forth clearly and systematically that imagination is both subjective and objective, that the object as experienced is, in plain terms, the object itself.

In 1790, Goethe published his *Metamorphosis of Plants* which represented a first step towards the overcoming of the "onlooker-consciousness" of conventional science. He started from the conviction that our senses as well as our intellect are gifts of nature, and that by observation we can awaken faculties, both perceptual and conceptual, that lay dormant within ourselves.

In observing plant forms he realised that they expressed a three-fold rhythm of expansion and contraction.

1. expansion from seed into leaf and leaf-bearing shoot;

2. contraction into calyx or involucre;

3. expansion into coloured petals;

4. contraction into pistil and stamens;

5. expansion of fertilised ovary into fruit;

6. contraction into seed.

And into this rhythmic life between contraction and expansion, between darkness beneath within the earth and light in the sky above, we must look to understand the plant in terms that are true to its living nature.

A modern exegesis of Goethe's methods in this field, aided by researches into projective geometry, is to be found in *The Plant Between Sun and Earth* by George Adams and Olive Whicher.

Goethe pursued a similar methodology in his exhaustive researches into the nature of light which led him to contest Newtonian theories based upon wavelengths and frequencies and splitting white light into components as a means to account for our experience of colour. Goethe challenged the Newtonian theories because he felt that they were mathematical theories based upon grossly limited evidence.

His own analysis of the spectrum was is in terms of the polarity of light and darkness, and he demonstrated that the spectral colours seen through a prism show only between areas of light and dark. Newton passed light through a pin hole before analysing it which Goethe considered artificial and self limiting in its conception and method, and the conclusions derived therefrom inflated from a special case.

One problem in the promulgation of Goethe's theory was that for it to be demonstrated it is not sufficient simply to read about it in a book but to actually undertake and experience the experiments oneself. As he said himself, "It is very difficult to pass on, for it needs not only to be read and studied but also to be done, and that has its difficulties."

A recognition of this problem has been met in the publication of a recent book upon the subject of Goethe's colour theory, *The Rediscovery of Color* by Heinrich O. Proskauer, where a small prism and experimental cards accompany the text so that the reader is able to experience something of Goethe's observations personally.

Goethe's ideas were dismissed as old-fashioned and non-mathematical when they first appeared in 1810 and have been largely ignored ever since. Nonetheless, the Massachusetts Institute of Technology Press reissued his *Theory of Colours* in 1970 partly as an historical curiosity but also with an acknowledgement of the grace and style of the exposition of an exemplary demonstration of systematic experiment with simple equipment, for Goethe had a passion for careful observation and accurate reporting.

He adheres closely to the ancient view, observed by Aristotle, that colour arises from the transition from brightness to darkness, and never even mentions the concept of frequency or wavelength. As Deane B. Judd observes in his introduction to the MIT edition, the advantage of trying to follow Goethe's explanations of colour phenomena is that by the time you have succeeded in doing so, your thoughts have become so divorced from the wavelength explanation of colour that you can begin to think about colour theory relatively unhampered by prejudice, either ancient or modern.

Insofar that when we try to predict what colours will be perceived to belong to objects under non-daylight conditions, we are likely to find that the wavelength explanation of colour falls down badly. It is therefore not beyond the bounds of possibility that Goethe's ideas may have been dismissed a little too readily, and might even provide a basis for future advance into the theory of colour.

It is Goethe's perceptions that are at the root of Owen Barfield's criticisms of the gigantic edifice of technical knowledge that is based upon ever more limiting types of "pin hole" perception – be it through the eyepiece of a microscope in one direction of magnitude, or that of a telescope in the other. It is based upon essentially "one-eyed" observations of the ever more remote, that can only be explained in ever more mathematical and abstract ways. Indeed, in the modern state of the art of electron microscopy and radio astronomy there is no longer any direct human observation but the computerised interpretation of mathematical data collected and recorded by electronic sensors. No sensory image is involved, save in simulated and artificial form. The whole process is one of the dehumanisation of perception.

# VII

## WHAT RUDOLF STEINER DID

The mode of phenomenological approach pursued and advocated by Goethe was a holistic one, based on intuitive perception and appreciation of the organic process and form-building functions of the creative powers to be observed in nature. When his collected works were being prepared for publication, the editorial responsibility for preparing the five volumes of scientific works fell to a young academic, Dr Rudolf Steiner (1861-1925).

So impressed was Steiner by Goethe's ideas that he decided to put them into practice, despite their having been dismissed as the speculations of an amateur by the scientific establishment. In doing so he jeopardised his career and reputation and eventually found that the only public platforms available to him were those beyond the fringe of academic respectability. He was aided in his early efforts by the Count and Countess Brockdorff, who were prominent Theosophists, and indeed for a brief period he accepted the presidency of the Theosophical Society in Germany, although his spiritual perceptions and affiliations were more closely concerned with western rather than oriental spiritual traditions.

Eventually he founded his own movement from which grew the Anthroposophical Society and a worldwide network of schools teaching by Steiner's principles. A similar network of schools, homes and residential villages has also been developed for handicapped children and adults. Biodynamic agriculture sprang from a course of lectures he gave in 1924 to a group of local farmers who were concerned, even then, about the consequences of "scientific" farming methods. Homeopathic clinics and hospitals have developed from his work with doctors, and his art of eurythmy has attracted much attention in the educational and therapeutic spheres. Training centres for teachers, agriculture, the arts and social work have also been established over the years.

The author of many pamphlets derived from shorthand notes of his lectures, his principal works are *Occult Science – an Outline* and *Knowledge of the Higher Worlds,†* while he has inspired a number of authors of scientific merit to develop various aspects of what he liked to term "spiritual science", of which *Man and Matter* by Ernst Lehrs and *The Rediscovery of Color* by Heinrich O. Proskauer and *The Plant Between Sun and Earth* by George Adams and Olive Whicher are notable examples – all stemming from the Goethean scientific method.

It was to Steiner's Anthroposophical Society that Owen Barfield was attracted in 1922, and which continued to form the backbone of his thought, his writing, and his continuing dialogue with C.S.Lewis. It was, however, the heartfelt complaint of Barfield that he could never get Lewis to take Rudolf Steiner seriously, despite the fact that the arguments and discussions that Lewis found so interesting were based very much on Steiner's principles.

He found it particularly incomprehensible in one such as Lewis, whose scholarly discipline in all other matters was immaculate. Lewis would never have allowed any student or colleague to pass a value judgement on any writer that he had not fully and assiduously read. Yet he seemed quite capable of dismissing Steiner out of hand. Typical of his attitude was the backhanded compliment to Steiner's concern for organic farming

†Recently reissued under the titles *An Outline of Esoteric Science* and *How to know Higher Worlds* -- ed.

methods that he was a good man to consult on manure but not on God.

In the end Barfield put down this blindness on the part of Lewis and the rest of the intellectual establishment as evidence of "tabu". He thought there was no less strong word to account for it. A tabu is a convention that changes with the passing of time, and is usually concerned with codes of sexual or social behaviour; things that one cannot respectably talk about. Different codes or beliefs may be acceptable or not in different places and times. This current tabu Barfield saw as the belief that it was not "done" to assume that the material world derives from a spiritual basis – despite all religious lip service to the contrary. When someone like Goethe, or Steiner, tries to investigate the material world on the assumption that it demonstrates an interior spirituality then, in terms of the tabu, they are considered beyond the pale of discourse. And this despite the progress that has been made by followers of Steiner's methods in education, agriculture, or homeopathic medicine and so on.

# VIII

## THIS EVER DIVERSE PAIR

When Barfield found the time to put more of his ideas down in writing he produced an amusing semi-autobiographical book in 1950 entitled *This Ever Diverse Pair*. In this assorted collection of vignettes from a lawyer's life, he depicts himself as a split personality – Burden, the persona he finds himself adopting as a professional lawyer; and Burgeon, the more humane, somewhat vacillating inner man. Towards the end of the book the two disparate characters are seen to be attempting to integrate.

Behind its wit and humour this little book contains much personal wisdom in the form of a review of his own life. It is largely a coming to terms with the question why a young man whose whole purpose in life was directed towards literature, language and spiritual concerns, should have been forced by circumstances into the prosaic duties of a practising lawyer for most of his life.

At the end we see this as a realisation of what might from one point of view be regarded as "karma", or from another the one course that was destined to bring out the best from within himself. In other words, that his life circumstances are ordered by a wiser and higher intelligence, irrespective of some of his own beliefs and inclinations.

It is this realisation that concludes the book, together with the reconciliation of the two sides of himself that had hitherto been kept apart. It might also be noted that the realisation of 1950 indicated in *This Ever Diverse Pair* seems to have sparked off the creativity and opportunities for his voice to be heard in his later years. In other words, our outer circumstances depend on our inner conscious assumptions, far more than we may think. Hence the initiatory injunction above the portal of the Delphic Oracle: "Know Thyself!"

# IX

## WORLDS APART

*This Ever Diverse Pair* is an individual account of what is seen as part of a wider human dilemma in *Worlds Apart.* Here Barfield pursues the problem in the form of fictional dialogues or symposia of considerable intellectual strenuousness. In *Worlds Apart* he strives to bridge the gaps that have developed between the various specialisations in human knowledge.

It is a discussion hosted by a lawyer, and has as participants two professors, one of historical theology and ethics, and the other of physical science. They are joined by two young research scientists, one in biology and the other in aerospace technology. Also by a linguistic philosopher and a psychiatrist. The party is completed by a retired schoolmaster who is an advocate of Rudolf Steiner's world view. The aim is to find an approach to modern problems that reconciles the diverse views of reality that are assumed by different academic disciplines. Because the sheer bulk of human knowledge demands ever increasing specialisation does this mean that man is losing sight of the wholeness of life?

The anthroposophical view, which of course is closest to Barfield's heart, is represented by Sanderson, the retired school-master, but Barfield himself is also represented as chairing the discussion in the person of Burgeon. Barfield was quite fond of this character Burgeon, who was, in a sense, a higher aspect of his own character, as we have seen in *This Ever Diverse Pair.*

The greater part of the argument in *Worlds Apart* is carried by the two professors, Hunter, a professor of historical theology and ethics, and Brodie, a professor of physical science. These two represent the classical sides of human debate and speculation about fundamental issues. The other characters have less central roles. Upwater, the biologist, is there to represent conventional views of evolution, which Barfield felt to be in particular need of revision. Ranger, a young rocket station researcher, is plainly out of his depth in such philosophic company, and indeed hardly realises that there is a problem at all. Dunn, the linguistic philosopher, is another who can contribute very little to the symposium, largely because he regards most of what is being said as meaningless in terms of his own limited viewpoint. Burrow, the psychiatrist, also tends to be wallowing somewhat out of his depth, while assuming that all are in the shallows of his own clinical concepts and diagnoses. However, Barfield obviously felt that their viewpoints should be put forward, if only to demonstrate their limitations. The two professors, representing classical scientific method and the traditional humanities, are considerably less arrogant or ignorant in their appreciation of the fundamental issues.

In fact Brodie cooperates with Burgeon in conducting a genuine Socratic discourse for the benefit of most of the others in order to demonstrate the illogicality of contemporary "scientism", particularly as it applies to popular conceptions of the prehistoric world. These assume, for instance, that there was no human consciousness on Earth in ancient times because of the lack of a fossil record. This is an assumption that is at best unproven, because absence of evidence does not prove non-existence. All it can possibly "prove" is that there were no solid bodies as we know them today. In popular conceptions of the significance of molecular physics there is also an illogicality in the importance placed upon an alleged "real world" of atoms and molecules that appears to exist side by side, or behind, the world of our physical sense perceptions, an abstraction of mathematical probabilities in vast areas of nothingness that replaces the ordinary world of human consciousness about us. And in the field of popular astronomy mathematical projections of vast distances and time scales replace the indigo vault of the heavens perceived by the natural eyes of man.

There is no question that these worlds revealed by astronomy and physics are untrue. They have proved much of their validity by the acid test of technological achievement. However, central to all is the role of human consciousness without which none of this would exist. Or if it did would be unperceived. If there was no such thing as human consciousness, Barfield asks us to ponder on just what would exactly exist? How could the quantum world of the atoms of physical substance make itself apparent without our consciousness to perceive it? For the world in terms of Coleridge's Primary Imagination is a system of representations, of appearances, in which perception is an act of imagination; and imagination is a creative act. Without the latter, what could possibly exist? Would there be a "grey veil" of electromagnetic quanta in a force field sufficient to itself alone? Fascinating as mathematical speculations might be as to the origin of the physical universe, or the extent of its outermost bounds, without a perceiving or an indwelling consciousness they are meaningless. It follows that to all intents and purposes investigation of the universe must centre upon man.

And one does not have to go to the far astronomical or subatomic limits to see this. It is enough to consider the comparatively recent palaeontological scenario, say in the time of the dinosaurs. Many pictures and models may be found in books and museums that purport to show what life was like in those times. It is of course admitted that these projections are conjectural, but this appears very much in the small print, and the impression given is that all that is shown is part and parcel of proven scientific fact. However, if we remove the factor of human consciousness and perception, nothing that is depicted in those prehistoric panoramas could possible have existed. The best that can be said is that if a human being, with the conscious perceptions of a modern man, had been there at that time, then possibly it might have appeared to him something like this. Barfield's point is that if no human being had been there it would not have appeared at all. Which is not to say that nothing would have existed, (he is not a Berkeleian idealist), but he does ask that we be honest about what might have been there, and how it would have appeared to whom.

Furthermore, popular "scientism", that passes as the prevailing common sense of our day, (just as a flat earth or the burning of witches appeared commonsensical to those of an earlier day), makes two major unproven assumptions:

i)that no intelligent life existed in prehistoric times;

ii)that the physical laws that condition the world today were the same then as they are now, unchanging through the millennia.

It is the function of Sanderson to sketch in, in his allegedly unscientific and inexpert Goethean way, an alternative to these speculative assumptions that are passed off in our times as established fact.

He gives an early indication of this in an early part of the seminar when he responds to the enthusiasm of the space researcher Ranger by saying that he cannot get very excited about the prospect of getting further and further into space, because he is there already! This pulls the others up short for a moment, but when challenged to explain this apparently nonsensical remark he withdraws it, apologising for appearing to be needlessly provocative. He then lets the others get on with their slow progress of discussion until he comes in again at the end with a detailed exposition of his alternative theories based upon a different way of looking at things and of investigating the phenomena of the world about us.

These theories are based upon the view that human consciousness is evolving and that the process is traceable through the changing use of language. At his present stage it is not only possible but essential for man to break out from the sense of isolation that his temporary immersion into materialism has caused. This has been a necessary phase, particularly acute over the past three or four hundred years. The next stage is an awakening to the spiritual world in all its range of expression about us. This includes not only recognition of our own spiritual being but of other spiritual beings that surround and dwell within the Earth.

This is too much for most of the others, whose assumptions do not permit them even to consider such matters. It is a demonstration of the "tabu" that Barfield describes elsewhere; a self imposed blindness to any reality beyond the physical world, even when that reality can be demonstrated by examination of the processes of the physical world, as in plant morphology or the behaviour of light as investigated by Goethe.

Even Hunter, whom, as a historian and student of theology and ethics, one might assume to be open to such a view, reacts strongly to these propositions. He is appalled by what he regards as a "clairvoyant" means of investigation, and the assumed possibility that consciousness might exist beyond the limits of the physical body. This distaste is not just a reaction to the lunatic fringe. Rather is it a common, and in some ways healthy assumption that individual spiritual integrity is somehow very closely bound up with a specific location in a physical body. To abandon this physical grounding is to risk becoming attenuated into some kind of rootless spook, a prey to whatever spectral wind might blow. However, Burgeon asserts that this natural fear is based upon an illusion – the concept of a mind sitting safely inside a cranium looking out through its perceptual windows onto a mindless universe, with which it has no connection except through the physical senses.

Also, the spiritual "integrity" or spiritual solitude which is apparently so prized is indeed something of a dangerous curse. It menaces the future of civilisation, and has caused a systematic cutting of traditional links with the old world of spiritual beings. It is now essential that we make a start by recognising the Earth itself to be an organism of conscious beings and not an inert mass of mindless matter.

Sanderson goes on to assert that release from this subjective prison comes only by death or by initiation. This implies that physical death will ultimately be followed by reincarnation for a further phase of evolutionary experience. Initiation on the other hand is a natural growth in spiritual stature that transcends current limitations of physical perception. However, it is only comparatively rare souls who have anything like open vision. These tend to form a body of revelation to which students seeking the wider vision are attracted. One example of such a soul, in Sanderson's view, was Rudolf Steiner.

Professor Hunter reacts in the way of a traditional theologian, and describes Sanderson's attitude as one that is best fitted by the Inquisitor's description of Protestantism: "a diabolical pride masquerading as a saintly humility". He goes on to add however that most modern materialists do not even bother to set up the masquerade! Sanderson sees no conflict between his spiritual evolutionary theme and accepted religious belief, and indeed Barfield himself, whose views are largely those of Sanderson, became a member of the Anglican communion.

# X

## UNANCESTRAL VOICE

These elements are further pursued in *Unancestral Voice*, together with an interesting description of inner communication with a spiritual being. This occurs in a perfectly natural way by use of the intuitive and imaginative faculties that need have caused no alarm to Professor Hunter with his fears of trance mediumship, astral projection or abnormal states of consciousness. In this account, which must surely have a strong autobiographical element, despite his assertion to the contrary in a recorded interview, Owen Barfield cites as a principal authority the work of a sixteenth century Jewish rabbi, Joseph Karo. This Qabalistic rabbi, like Barfield himself, is a lawyer who is also deeply concerned with the spiritual side of life. He kept a diary known as the *Maggid Mesharim* in which he recorded the details of communication with a kind of inner voice that spoke within his mind in periods of silence and solitude. Although, as some of his contemporaries bear witness, sometimes it inspired Karo spontaneously to speak its words.

The inner voice was identified with various possible sources by Rabbi Karo and his associates – as an angel; as the "Shekinah" or presence of God; as the spirit of the *Mishnah* (a record of traditional written teachings). In modern times alternative labels might have been accorded it – the subconscious; the "active imagination"; Coleridge's "repetition in the finite mind of the infinite I AM"; or even a dominating mother imago. Burgeon, the modern protagonist of this story, determines to cast aside other people's prejudices and to try it for himself.

First of all he needs to go through something of an internal confrontation, as his *alter ego* Burden attempts to pour all sorts of commonsensical cold water upon the project. However, Burgeon refuses to be put off. At first his contact with the Meggid takes the form of realisations that come into his mind when he is meditating about some general problem. One instance is his concern about the generation gap between post-war youth and its elders. Another is a celebrated issue of the time, the court case over the alleged obscenity or literary merit of *Lady Chatterley's Lover.* In the conceptions brought to his mind by the Meggid these are but contemporary symptoms of an impending phase change in the evolution of human consciousness. An old age is going out and a new age is coming in.

In the time since *Unancestral Voice* was written "New Age" speculation has become almost commonplace but this was less so in 1965 when Barfield's book was published. He uses the type of terminology favoured by Rudolf Steiner in his designation of the different forces acting upon human consciousness. Thus the period going out is represented as being the Gabriel age, and the phase coming in as the Michael. The names are derived from the traditional major archangels. The transition from one age to another is complicated by conflicting forces of disruption, designated as those of Ahriman, which represents the forces of die-hard conservatism, and of Lucifer, which represents new energies and attitudes trying to come in too fast. This accounts for the conflict between the generations that came to a particular crisis in the 1960's, and the *Lady Chatterley* case also encapsulated much of the current confusion. D.H.Lawrence correctly realised that the old mind dominated ways of thought were deadening, but his error was to assume that all could be put right by a rush into sensuality. Certainly the focus of creative expression has been changing in that direction, and Lawrence condemned the old conceptions as "sex in the head", which includes the transcendent medieval imagery of Dante and the divine beloved, Beatrice.

Barfield refers to C.S.Lewis' *Allegory of Love* to illustrate some of the issues involved. Following upon the early medieval vision we see sex beginning to be focused in the heart in the elaborations of courtly love. And in the wider term creative art begins to be applied more to the depiction of the human as opposed to the divine. In the more recent turn of the spiral creativity is coming in to human expression further down in the archetypal human frame, hence the emphasis on physical sexuality. The modern hero and heroine express themselves as much through the loins as through the head or heart. However, as Barfield succinctly points out, it is not likely that enthusiastic copulation is all that is required to set things right!

The way ahead is demonstrated in a symbolic dream that comes to Professor Hunter in the postscript to *Worlds Apart*. In this lucid vision (which he was presumably not too horrified to receive as a symptom of "clairvoyance" or altered states of consciousness), he finds himself outside great symbolic gates, where he meets three strange human figures.

The first has a hollow box in place of a head, and great light is pouring through the eye holes. It represents "subjective idealisam".

The second has a great lion's head with a mane extending out like radiating sun's rays. This represents "the Key to the Kingdom". It is the expression of our own spirituality and creativity as a centre of radiance.

The third figure has no head at all, and represents "the Kingdom" itself. It implies that the "internal", the inside of one's head, is co-extensive with the infinite universe.

Following upon these colloquies with the Meggid, Burgeon discusses the implications while on a sea voyage with a Christian and a Buddhist. Much of their discussion revolves about an evolutionary view of history and whether, if it is true, it is "driven from the inside", by consciousness. In the words of the Meggid, that "the interior is anterior". As he converses with his ship companions Burgeon finds that, as was recorded by Kara, the Qabalistic rabbi, words seem to be coming to him of their own volition. He is becoming a voluntary mouthpiece for the Meggid, or, as he puts it:

> That the Meggid himself was now speaking in him. How long that had been going on, he could not say, for it was definitely "in" and not "through"; there was no question of his being used as a sort of microphone; and yet it was almost as much like hearing someone else speak as it was like speaking.

He finds himself uttering, "with all the confidence of personal experience", things that he could not possibly have known from personal experience, because he had not lived them, let alone "lived up" to them! This comprises the second stage of his contact with the Meggid.

The third stage develops at a scientific conference. Here the discussion revolves around the implications of quantum mechanics, and Burgeon finds himself unable to intervene because of his lack of scientific knowledge. There is, however, a young scientist on the platform, whose ideas, at least in embryo, appear to lie close to his own. The young man has something of a chilly reception from sections of the audience and Burgeon wishes that he could somehow help him in the ensuing discussion.

The gist of the talk by the young nuclear physicist, Kenneth Flume, is the problem that is currently posed by the investigation of subatomic particles. These have become increasingly difficult to conceptualise, and there has been considereable difficulty in deciding whether to regard them as particles or as waves. The genereally accepted solution (if such a compromise can be called a solution) is to regard them as particles like packets of waves, which are called quanta. Niels Bohr, the pioneer atomic physicist, has suggested that if we are indeed to conceptualise these quanta then we need to visualise not one but two models in parallel, one picturing them as particles and the other picturing them as waves. Meanwhile the phenomena continue to be interpreted mathematically in terms that become increasingly meaningless to the majority of mankind. This is further complicated in that as soon as one set of "ultimate particles" is analysed, a further set is discovered, involving concepts such as zero magnitude.

Flume suggest that this is possibly a quest for knowledge that is rushing down a blind alley. That if it becomes impossible to conceptualise a situation then the way is blocked for further progress, because the intuitive and conceptualising powers of the human mind are denied any pabulum to work upon. He tentatively suggests that instead of a continued mathematical quest for the ever more minute and fundamental particle, that the way forward might be the application of the imagination to modes of function and purpose. He concedes that this may seem an unlikely route to most of his audience but the crisis is such that some radical new direction seems imperative, and so no possible avenue of investigation should be left unexplored.

The ultimate destination to which such a line of thought may well lead is not lost upon Burgeon, who is familiar with Goethe's approach to phenomena. Goethe's method, both in terms of the structure of light and in the morphology of plant growth, leads naturally to an appreciation of the "etheric" realm wherein the forms of nature are shaped and conceived. And these are open to human perception with the requisite training, the cleansing and opening of the appropriate doors of perception. This will lead ultimately to the discovery of a different type of entity from the sub-atomic particle, to the hierarchies of form building intelligence that create the particles and use them as building blocks in the structure of the life forms of nature. Thus everything in the universe, even the most seemingly inanimate, is a mode of life, although with an ego placed differently in relation to its form than is the case with the human (where it coalesces with the body).

Naturally, without going even this far, the speaker's suggestions have moved into realms that are far too speculative for the majority of his audience. He is subjected to vociferous attack and finds some difficulty in coping with it particularly as he is himself only tentatively beginning to grope his way into this avenue of alternative thought. Burgeon feels that some kind of help is needed. This is beyond his own intellectual capabilities in such company, so it would seem to be a case for the wisdom of the Meggid. This is duly invoked, and he becomes aware of the Meggid's "approach" by a variety of subtle psychosomatic indicators to which he has become accustomed. Then, to his surprise, the Meggid seems to pass him by. And to his even greater surprise it makes contact directly with the speaker, inspiring him to formulate his final reply to the whole discussion. The form of this reply is very much like a challenge --and a challenge that extends from Einstein's ultimate objection to the way nuclear research was heading when, almost in despair, he asserted "God does not play dice".

The Meggid, through Flume, reminds his audience that the classical scientific search has been for the stable basis, the stable entities, that are fundamental to the processes of perpetual transformation that are observable in the world of phenomena. That the waters have been muddied by the introduction of field theory, which implies that the laws governing large scale phenomena are not necessarily those governing small scale phenomena. This has led to a dichotomy between defining the field as the behaviour of its constituent particles, or alternatively considering the behaviour of the particles to be determined by the field. Then the element of randomness had been brought in (to Einstein's dismay), which implies that ultimately all the structure we see about us is based upon chance – the average result of a system of irrational irregularities, definable only in terms of "fields of probability".

Although this might be mathematically consistent, it implies abandoning the age old quest for stable entities. It is at root a renunciation of the principle of causality. Reminding his hearers of the ideals of those who began the scientific revolution, Flume insists that the phenomenon of "the random, the fortuitous, the unexplained" is a challenge for us to seek out the causes in some new, hitherto unexplored, domain. In the processes of transformation that are observed in the apparent discontinuity of motion, where particles appear randomly to disappear, or to appear elsewhere, it is not enough to retreat behind mathematical barriers, avoiding the concept that creation is being operated in another domain, the appreciation of which would reveal the true transformative relationship between the whole and the part. To try to do otherwise is to try to understand the architecture of the house by analysing the bricks.

Finally he makes a direct challenge: "What kind of source can there be for the complex interacting of rhythms of energy, of which we now find that the physical universe exists? What other can it be than a system of non-spatial relationships between hierarchies of energetic beings?" This implies the need for using the imagination in a new way, which many of the audience find amusing or embarrassing. Yet this may be the only way to obtain perceptive access to the realm of these causative entities and forces. Indeed, the way forward may not be a process of thinking *about* them but endeavouring to think *with* them, in their particular mode of activity, so that their energy informs our thought. This indeed is what is already occurring in the case of Flume although he does not yet realise it. And it has all been happening in a perfectly natural way, not through ecstatic trances or oracular phenomena of a bygone age, when man was incapable of direct personal intuitive perception. Then they had to depend on the immersion of the consciousness more deeply into the preternatural environment at a time when the individuality was less well defined.

This modern mode of mentation might be called the operation of Pure Reason, and, like the power of the Primary Imagination in perception, it is part of the grand philosophic design of Coleridge which he never systematically completed. Owen Barfield did his best to reveal it as a coherent organism in his final book *What Coleridge Thought,* a project that he had first tentatively approached in a lecture of 1932 on *The Philosophy of Samuel Taylor Coleridge*, reprinted in *Romanticism Comes of Age.* Reason, for Coleridge, is not something to be found manifesting in human beings, it is something *in* which human beings, and the whole of nature, are manifest. It is not merely a part of the function of the individual mind. It is that spiritual whole in which the individual mind (along with all other individual minds) subsists. It is in fact as much an objective as a subjective reality. It is, to quote his term, "superindividual".

We may from this perhaps glean some clue as to the true nature of the Meggid, whom Burgeon was ultimately to address in time honoured fashion as "Master", only to be gently reminded that the Meggid was but a servant of others, all of whom were servants of one master of them all, who in turn was the servant of all of them, as indeed the Meggid was servant of Burgeon, as he himself of his readers. And in an encoded farewell salutation

he signed himself as "I am" and "Yours", combining the intimacy of a love letter with the fiery statement of identity from
the Source of All that spoke from the burning bush.

# XI

## ORPHEUS

Much of Owen Barfield's writing is densely packed intellectual argument, and the closest he comes to purely imaginative work is in these conversation pieces. However, he did write a poetic drama, *Orpheus,* in the early 1940's, at the instigation of C.S.Lewis, which is pure mythopoeia, or what we could equally call magically loaded writing, for the performance of it could provide an initiatory experience to participants and audience alike, if appropriately performed. Or if read in a meditative fashion, dwelling with deep feeling upon the visual images, could have a profound effect upon the individual reader.

C.S.Lewis thought very highly of it, not only as poetry, but for its mythopeoic element, and wrote to Barfield, "I await with great interest the public reaction to a work˙which has influenced me so deeply ..." However, public reaction has been scant because of the play's limited exposure. It received a week of performances at the Little Theatre, Sheffield, in 1948, and would have disappeared from sight but for publication of the text in 1983 by the Lindisfarne Press (a small press dedicated to a fourfold programme of "the transformation of individual consciousness; the understanding of the inner harmony of the world's great religious traditions; the illumination of the spiritual dimensions of world order; and the creation of an ecologically and spiritually appropriate meta-industrial culture." These aims might well serve to summarise Owen Barfield's lifelong concerns).

An undated latter from C.S.Lewis records how disappointed he felt at the lack of any great acclaim for *Orpheus.* "It is better than I remembered. How can they *not* see?" However, thanks to the dedication and detective work of John C. Ulreich Jr. of the University of Arizona, it survived to be published. Ulreich records that his first reading of the play struck him with the force of a revelation; that here was Barfield's belief in the evolution of consciousness made flesh. By its very nature the play is capable of many levels of interpretation, and to attempt to describe it is to risk ignoring, distorting or destroying more than one illuminates. However, a broad story line may serve to help rather than hinder those who may find Barfield difficult, for much may be rendered plain in parable that seems obscure in abstraction.

In the opening scene the Nereids, the fifty daughters of the ancient sea god Nereus, are seen at play. There is a certain macabre element to this in that they are sporting with the headless corpse of a drowned sailor. However, this serves at one level to foreshadow the eventual sacrificial death of Orpheus, and also to remind us of the significant encounter that Nereus once had with Heracles, the archetypal human hero. Heracles found the sea god sleeping and bound him fast until he revealed the secret of the golden apples that grow in the gardens of the far west, watched over by a dragon. In this parallel myth, the formless sea of primal consciousness, with its ever changing shapes, had been conquered by the spiritual principle of human individuality expressed as hero. This theme is repeated, after another fashion, in the action of the play, where Orpheus appears on the shore and identifies one of the Nereids as the object of his desire, calling her forth from the watery element to join him on the dry land.

At first she is incapable of self-conscious identification and refers to herself in the third person, but she develops her individuality as Orpheus sings to her about all the things of nature. He also teaches her memory, which is the basis of ratiocination and understanding. She begins to realise the nature of permanence, symbolised in the difference between the soil of the earth and the sand of the seashore. The sand runs through her hands, leaving no trace of its passing, while the loam leaves it mark on the hands that have held and shaped it. Euridice attains full self-consciousness when Orpheus gives her the gift of a mirror, "the eye aware of itself". But as he does so, a serpent rears up from a nearby tree root. This frightens Euridice but Orpheus puts the serpent to sleep and Euridice, with her new found self-aware-ness, goes to adorn herself. This runs parallel to the Garden of Eden story although with a rather different emphasis. As Euridice goes she throws her scarf to Orpheus, who buries his face in it, which also indicates an element of self-blinding or limitation. Orpheus, insofar as he represents the spiritual principle, under-goes limitation in the very act of bringing individualisation to the lower consciousness.

The spiritual principle represented by Orpheus is also repre-sented in his half-brother Aristaeus, who now appears. Aristaeus and Orpheus are both sons of Apollo, the sun god, which gives them their spiritual dimension. Orpheus however has for a mother one of the Muses, (Calliope, who presides over heroic poetry), while the mother of Aristaeus is a water nymph, Cyrene. It fol-lows that, of the two, Aristaeus is more naturally earth-oriented than the celestially engendered Orpheus. However, as sons of a common father, the incidents that befall them are similar in na-ture, although differently expressed. Aristaeus is depicted as more of a rustic character than the wandering musician Orpheus. His functions are to attend the earthly altars of Apollo and to be a husbandman of the Earth. In particular he is custodian of a swarm of bees, honey being sacred to Apollo. The bees also have a spiritual function in being intermediaries between the worlds. Aristaeus, however, is currently suffering from a double mis-fortune. This also resonates with events in the story of Orpheus. While Orpheus has been calling forth and individualising

Euridice from the formless waters, Aristaeus has lost his swarm of bees. Also, his beloved son, Actaeon, has been torn apart as a consequence of gazing upon the goddess Artemis bathing.

Euridice then returns, adorned with all the sophistication of a fine Greek lady, to call Orpheus into the love bower that is prepared for them. In following her into the bower Orpheus is diverted from his intention of killing the sleeping serpent. They retire to make love, the ultimate polarisation and at-one-ment of the celestial Orpheus and the lower world Euridice. Euridice, however, interrupts their lovemaking the more greatly to savour the nuances of a loving relationship by temporary parting, and in wandering out of the bower comes upon Aristaeus, who, inflamed by the atmosphere of love that has permeated the scene (rather like little Cupids in the form of invisible bees) tries to make love to her himself, and upon being denied attempts to use force. In her attempt to escape, Euridice stumbles upon the serpent, who wakes and stings her, and she falls unconscious and is dragged down to Hades, the lower world of the dead.

In the second Act Euridice is at the gates of Hades, confronted by Charon the ferryman. Charon has a problem in that it is not clear as to whether Euridice is really dead or merely sleeping. There is a dispute between the god of the underworld, Hades, (after whom the place is named), and his consort Persephone. Persephone herself is a mediator between worlds, as she spends only half the year in the underworld. For the other half of the year she returns to her mother, the Earth goddess Demeter, bringing with her the growth of vegetation. Hades is naturally suspicious of all water nymphs following his unfortunate experience with the nymph Arethusa, who in the form of an underground stream, discovered the whereabouts of Persephone and told it to Demeter when the Earth goddess was searching and grieving for her lost daughter. In this respect water nymphs play a similar role to the bees, who are here described as having the function of bringing sunlight to hell and taking something back to earth in return, presumed to be some precious essence of the virtuous dead. It is also states that the bees can indeed be forms of Proteus, the primeval water god, "the life of light undarkened into form". It is plain that Hades is deeply afraid of all these elements of the higher worlds penetrating his world of mechanic restriction, even though they include his own wife. He insists that Euridice should be chained in a hall with the spirits of the damned, but Persephone insists that her destination is the freedom of Elysium, the dwelling place of the spirits of the blessed.

Meanwhile Orpheus in the upper world of earth is lamenting the loss of Euridice, she "who drew down his music to the Earth". He is tempted to regret the calling down of the heavenly muses to be enchanted in the solid sphere of earthly form but puts this behind him and sings instead of a dream, in which Persephone appeared to him and showed him a higher vision of nature and of the Earth. On concluding his song he finds that he has attracted all the animals of the Earth about him by his singing, as once he attracted Euridice from the sea. He seeks to help them in recognisance of their having saved him from his solitary melancholy. His voice is their bridge toward a higher form of life expression and they in turn contribute their own special wisdom to him.

The serpent and the swan with its serpentine neck speak of their embodiment of a polar relationship. One is the bright pole and the other the dark pole that is epitomised in the story of Zeus, who has appeared as a swan to Leda and ravished her, to bring forth on the one hand the bright Helen and on the other the dark Clytemnestra. The bull reveals himself as the embodiment of star music within the Earth. The ass, like Balaam's ass, reveals himself as obstinately wise, obeying higher guidance despite the blows of expediency. The eagle is revealed as mediator between Heaven and Earth, and the bearer of Ganymede, the cup bearer to the gods, who is himself likened to a human eagle. The lamb is revealed as the willing sacrifice, constantly kissing the Earth in its feeding, and then giving to man first its wool and then its flesh. The nightingale sings a song of wisdom of the heart, to be concerned with the woes of others rather than of oneself. She is represented in the myth of Philomel, who was raped by her sister's husband before being turned into a nightingale; and she sings not of her own woe but of the sorrow and misfortune of her betrayed sister. Finally the lion speaks with authority for all of the animals, calling for Orpheus to break into the underworld and give the gift of his heavenly music to Persephone, and to follow the wisdom of his own heart. This seems a strange directive to the spiritually oriented Orpheus, for the human heart is a wayward guide, but it is the lessons of the heart that the spirit has to learn, and is arguably the reason for its involvement in form. By the polar interchange, spirit gives identity to form, and form brings compassion to the spirit.

Orpheus thus wends his way to Hades on behalf of the animals and to seek out Persephone, the goddess of the underworld, who yet also was she who brought to him, in sleep, the wondrous vision of a transformed Earth. Hades, which we enter with Orpheus in Act III, is rather like an efficient corporation or corporate state in the world we know. All the denizens are persuaded into thinking that they live in the best of all possible worlds and that they should be grateful for their hellish lot. Sisyphus is content to keep rolling his boulder everlastingly up hill, impressed with the idea of the dignity of labour. Tantalus, ever prevented from slaking his thirst, is content with the constant thrill of desire unsated. And the Danaids, with their leaking pitchers, are happy to be ever running to the spring of transient fashion, glad that their pitchers will soon empty themselves before they are carried too far. To emphasise this mechanic culture, all movements of the denizens of Hades appear jerky and automatic, like a badly synchronised film, and Hades himself is prone to address his subjects through loud and distorted amplification equipment. The howls of the hell hound Cerberus also sound very much like the squeals of electronic negative feedback. We are clearly not so far from Hades in our contemporary culture.

When Orpheus appears with his lyre, however, he awakens all the denizens of the underworld to their lost humanity. And he himself experiences a major awakening in that in his searching for Persephone he finds instead Euridice. A great mystery is involved here, it would seem, as the voice of Persephone bids Orpheus beware as he approaches the sleeping Euridice. Persephone covers her face as Orpheus reaches out to Euridice, and when he actually touches her Orpheus drops his lyre, which shatters at his feet. He has thus lost his celestial voice through the underworld reunion with Euridice. Euridice is awoken by his touch, and in the process of awakening, is vouchsafed a vision of stars, or star beings and goddesses, regarding each other with love and moving in stately dance. She wills and longs to become one with them, but finds there is a dreadful chasm between herself and this Elysian condition. As she wakes she is immediately enchained according to the edicts of Hades. Hell is full of laws, and its god loves to proclaim them. Persephone protests against this chaining of Euridice, and Hades gives Orpheus leave to break the chain, but subject to certain conditions. Euridice will be free to come and go but she will only be able to enter the heavenly realms with Orpheus at her side.

Persephone warns Orpheus and Euridice of the dangers that may befall them despite the apparent opportunity given them by

Hades, who has in fact become a subtle tempter. They will return to the upper world to do and suffer many things. They will
be together but it will not always seem so, as they go "through
doubt and dark". It is plain that this freedom that they have been
given is very dangerous, and Hades relies on their abusing it.
Already in fact we have the feeling that Orpheus has forgotten
his mission on behalf of the animals as a consequence of regain-
ing Euridice. Persephone then leads them out of Hades, Orpheus
following immediately behind her, with Euridice behind him,
and Persephone warns Orpheus that he may not turn to gaze at
Euridice but must keep his eyes on the goddess who walks before him. This injunction meets the test when Hades send his
spy, the night hawk Ascalaphos, to follow them, imitate
Euridice's voice, and tempt Orpheus to turn his head. A great
conflict is induced within Orpheus as a result of this. He is as-
sailed with reproaches, apparently from Euridice, that he no
longer loves her. He is torn between obeying the natural
promptings of his heart, as instructed by the animals, or following the instructions of the goddess. At the point where Persephone
enters the upper world ahead of them, and so disappears from
sight, Orpheus turns back to look at Euridice. She is forthwith
dragged back down to Hades and Orpheus is left with nothing
but a fragment of the chain that bound her.

The fourth Act commences with Aristaeus, Orpheus's *alter
ego*, standing at the source of the stream of waters of life that
runs to the formless ocean. In parallel action with Orpheus's
loss of Euridice, all the bees of Aristaeus have become diseased
and died. He stands by the side of the river, reviewing his destiny as a priest of his father Apollo on earth. This priesthood has
been particularly expressed by the honey produced by the bees.
This is various described as strands of the sun god's bright hair;
glory focused into taste; and liquid light charmed into the golden

wonder of the honeycomb. He has, to an extent, betrayed his trust in his attempt to force himself upon Euridice against her will, just as Orpheus has fallen short by losing sight of his wider commitment to the animals in is absorbing passion for Euridice. Seeking the help and consolation of his mother, Cyrene, the water nymph, Aristaeus descends into the waters of the river, just as a satyr, attendant upon the Maenads, arrives. The satyr and the Maenads perform a wild dance that is also a mock mystery drama. It celebrates Zeus making love to Semele and begetting upon her a child. This is produced as a corn dolly with a red rose heart.

Then the jealous Hera is represented as appearing and throwing the baby to the Titans. To commemorate this the straw doll is torn apart by the Maenads and the satyr, as Zeus takes and conceals on his person the red rose heart. They then enact Zeus appearing to Semele, who is blasted by the unveiled glory of the god. This gives birth to Dionysus, who is god of the vine and of the honey bee, and represented by the reconstructed corn dolly, complete with red rose heart. The wild women of the Maenads now seek a real sacrificial victim with which to celebrate the Dionysian revel. At this point Orpheus enters, but his lyre having been broken in the underworld, he carries only the chain of Euridice. He attempts to sing but is capable only of banalities.

The satyr mocks him and his false notes, insisting that true sweetness is to be found only in the powers of the earth. That nature grieves not, but is an ever changing cycle where nothing lasts or repeats itself. True loyalty is thus not to some ideal or spiritual abstraction but in living full bloodedly with the lusts of the earth. (This is much in line with the message of D.H.Lawrence and *Lady Chatterley's Lover* that Barfield discussed in *Worlds Apart*.) Under pressure from the satyr Orpheus throws away the chain, and as it sinks into the river he is immediately stricken

with guilt at having further disobeyed an injunction of the goddess Persephone, who had told him it was to be kept for a specific
purpose. He now finds that he has lost even what little powers
of song that remained to him. The satyr counsels him to make
sacrifice to "the earth born god", Dionysus, and that he should
give himself to the wild women of the Maenads in whom is to
be found the might of the earth. Orpheus however denies this as
a remedy. He has lost his divine voice and celestial harmony
because he has betrayed the Muses, who have fled from mankind as a result of man's false thinking. The great god Pan is
capable only of curing unhappy men by turning them into happy
animals.

At this the satyr throws at him the slanderous jibe that he has
coupled with animals – a reference to the old tradition of angels,
or "sons of god", falling from heaven and coupling with the
daughters of primeval men. And if this is not the case then he is
guilty of trying to set himself up higher than the god who sprang
from the earth, which brings the fury of the Maenads upon him.
They tear him limb from limb; his head is thrown into the waters, while the wild women, and the animals who accompany
them, devour the rest of his body.

We now follow Aristaeus beneath the waters, in an action
which occurs simultaneously with the preceding scene. Slowly
Aristaeus gains conscious awareness of the underwater world.
He sees a nymph pouring wine drop by drop from a cup, which
gives the principle and capability of form to the flowing waters.
His mother Cyrene then utters a prophetic vision that declares
that the ancient water god Proteus, who is all creatures except
himself, and is life drifting from shape to shape, ever flowing
and flowing away, must be fixed in form, using the chain that
was forged in Hades, and which Persephone had placed into the
care of Orpheus when he struck it from the body of Euridice.

The surrounding nymphs think they have found the chain, which Orpheus has thrown into the waters. They find instead however his head, which is still speaking of Euridice. They reverently let it drift downstream to the sea. Having done this they find the chain, which is given to Aristaeus to use as his mother has prophetically bidden, to bind Proteus into form.

In its juxtaposition of symbols, the cup of form-giving wine, the head of Orpheus, the chain given to Aristaeus, we have various ways of expressing the form-giving powers of the spirit acting upon the natural formlessness of nature and collective ground of consciousness. In *What Coleridge Thought,* which can act as an explanatory commentary to the play, as the play in turn can illustrate the book, this is *natura naturans* (creative powers of nature) giving life and organisation to *natura naturata* (the forms of nature), which is otherwise capable only of mechanism. At another level Orpheus and Aristaeus each represent aspects of the Reason, the divine principle in man, the neo-Platonic *nous,* the *lux interna,* the divine spark, the Promethean fire, that gives spiritual individuality and integrity and raises man above the animal condition. Euridice represents the soul, which is capable of being individualised from a common ground of conscious potentiality, and in union with the spiritual principle, entering Elysium.

The final scene of the play takes place after Aristaeus has bound Proteus, the teeming formless life force, into spiritual forms and inter-relationships. This is celebrated by the willing sacrifice of the great black star bull. The satyr, the Maenads, and the animals are in attendance, all of them transformed from their savagery since their dismemberment of Orpheus and partaking of his flesh and blood in a mystic communion of the Dionysian mysteries raised to a spiritual level. Aristaeus confesses his own shortcomings in all that has gone before by in effect calling down the music of the spheres into the pulsing rhythm and clamour of the blood, the alien strengths of animal lust. The willing sacrifice of the bull marks the transmutation of these lower forms and forces. As the sacrificial blow is struck, in a scene that calls to mind the ancient Mithraic mystery drama, the buzzing of many bees is heard, swarming up through cracks in the Earth, their bodies radiant with light. The entrails of the bull become a source of glowing light, fermenting with glory. And the voices of Euridice and Orpheus are heard ascending to Elysium.

The implications of this scene unite Christian and pagan visions of the glorification of the world and the re-establishment of the earthly paradise. This is aptly reflected in the Mithraic symbolism, a mystery system that ran orthodox Christianity close to being accepted as the official religion of the Roman empire. In Barfield's view, the Christian mythos would have been preserved for all mankind in some form or another, even if the events of the life and death of Jesus of Nazareth had been expunged from all the records, as those of the parallel Gnostic or Mithraic systems have been all but completely destroyed. They all celebrate a cosmic turning point in the history of human consciousness upon the planet, which was the possibility of individualisation by the human soul and spirit.

It would serve no useful purpose to try to add commentary upon commentary in further analysis of Barfield's work. It is all there in the texts themselves and the astute and interested reader will be better employed going to the actual source rather than to rely upon our own leaking bucket. Whether taking the imaginative approach of the poetic mystery drama, or the rational analysis of *What Coleridge Thought,* they are but in their turn the modern representatives of an ancient line of tradition that Coleridge himself studied while still at school, ranging from

Plato and Plotinus to Marsilio Ficino, Giordano Bruno and Jacob Boehme. That company that Barfield describes as:

> That philosophical stream of thought which has not ceased to irrigate the culture of the West, and in particular its literature, art and theory of art, since it first began to flow, though it has percolated underground for much longer periods than those during which it has watered the surface.

# XII

## THE SILVER TRUMPET

This fairy story, ostensibly written for children, comes very early in Owen Barfield's published work, in 1925, just three years after he had formally affiliated himself to the anthroposophical teachings of Rudolf Steiner. It deserves some close attention insofar that if *Orpheus* represents a codification of his metaphysical and philosophical ideas in dramatic form in his mature years, then *The Silver Trumpet* fulfils a similar function in his salad days.

Whether or not any such intention was intentional we may never know, and either way it makes little difference if the material was filtered through his conscious mind or his subconscious. However, given the dedication of the Anthroposophical movement to education and the imaginative development of the child it may perhaps be no great surprise that Barfield's first venture into creative writing was a fairy story for children.

At the same time we should not forget the respect within the same tradition for what have been called "ludibria" – that is to say, apparently fantastic stories that contain serious teaching of a metaphysical nature. This was a feature of the seventeenth century Rosicrucian tradition, with *The Chymical Wedding of Christian Rosencreutz* being a prime example. In ancient times the classic example is Apuleius of Madaura's *Golden Ass*, an apparently comic novel with pious interludes that contain much coded teaching about the Mysteries of Isis and Osiris. Closer to home, Goethe himself contributed to the genre with a story called *The Green Snake and the Beautiful Lily*.

We are entitled therefore to suspect that *The Silver Trumpet* might well prove to be another work along these lines. Indeed there is much, even on the surface, that is reminiscent of Steiner's teachings about polarity of forces, whether conceived as light and dark, (the basis of Goethe's colour theory) or more sophisticatedly as spirit and matter, or sun and earth – an important anthroposophical text being *The Plant Between Sun and Earth,* a treatise demonstrating plant morphology to be a development from these complementary principles. Similarly, great attention has been paid by followers of Steiner into projective geometry, a branch of mathematics developed at much the same time as 19th century romanticism out of earlier work by the mystic and mathematician Pascal. It develops a network of multidimensional forms from the dual relationship between a point and infinity. Keller von Asten's *Encounters with the Infinite* and Olive Whicher's practical workbook *Projective Geometry* are anthroposophical texts expounding its principles.

It is therefore perhaps not suprising to find that Barfield's *The Silver Trumpet* starts with the birth of identical twins. Although they love each other more than anything else in the world, and are therefore inseparable, a certain dichotomy develops between them. One has a tendency towards being something of a goody two-shoes whilst the other is drawn towards being something of a scheming cross-patch. We would hesitate to assign them to good and evil, as this is too stark an opposition, but a closer correspondence might be found in Steiner's conception of opposing principles that he calls Lucifer and Ahriman. Lucifer tends towards light and Ahriman towards darkness – Lucifer signifies progress and Ahriman reaction – both are needful expressions of life and become evil only if one outbalances the other.

The girl twins are baptised Violetta and Gambetta and as such are completely indistinguishable from one another. There is a certain benevolent power in the background that is responsible for this situation, a white witch known as Miss Thomson, who in the traditional role of fairy godmother places three gifts upon them:

a) that they should be as alike as two peas;

b) that they should love each other more than all else in the world;

c) somewhat more enigmatically, that as long as one of them is living, both shall BE.

The implications of this last cryptic remark are not revealed until towards the end of the story.

As a result of these gifts their somewhat self seeking mother says that she is sure both children will be very happy, although Miss Thomson advises her not to be too sure about that. One has the impression that the queen's invitation of the fairy godmother stemmed from hopes of what might be gained from her, rather than for her own sake, and thus any blessings she brings may contain certain lessons to learn.

The identical appearance of the two girls causes some confusion at first but this is resolved by a leading courtier, the Lord High Teller of the Other from Which, whom some think a fool but who is in fact something of a wise man. He realises that whilst they may look alike on the outside, on the inside the girls are completely different – indeed one might say polar opposites. He notices this because Violetta is naturally sympathetic to the plight of others, while Gambetta is not naturally so, appearing more worldly wise, to put it in the most charitable terms.

The Lord High Teller of the Other from Which is also well acquainted with the magical power of names, and renames the two girls Violet and Gamboy, after which their opposing characteristics become more apparent to all and sundry.

Whether there is some coded message for us in the actual change of name is open to conjecture, but it is worth remarking that Barfield's great preoccupation at this time was on the emotional charge and changing meaning in evolutionary time of different words. This was the subject of his B.Litt. dissertation, later published as *Poetic Diction* and of his popular early work *History in English Words,* whilst he had also made the acquaintance of J.R.R.Tolkien, who likewise had a strong personal and professional interest in the power of words.

The different attitudes of the two girls has its corresponding physical effect upon their faces. Gamboy's calculating attitude to life produces wrinkles and Violet's more sunny disposition produces dimples, but because of their inherent love for each other, the characteristic marks appear on both their faces. This means that Violet is not so beautiful as she might have been, and Gamboy is not so ugly as she might have been. As they grow up the two girls cannot bear to be out of each other's company although their opposite dispositions mean that they argue most of the time.

So things continue until one day a handsome young prince appears on the scene, clad in silver chain mail and blowing a silver trumpet. The appearance of the prince and the sound of his trumpet call has a different effect upon each of the girls.

The sight of him causes Violet to break out into song, as she does whenever she is excited. The song has a certain spiritual ambience, its words being "Create a sensation of glory – all in the land of Judaea." Gamboy has the more down to earth reaction. To her jaundiced eye the silver knight is bound to prove to be just another  conceited young man - like all the rest!

The trumpet's call causes Violet to be transported into a reverie wherein she feels as if she is floating at the bottom of a great sea. It causes Gamboy to lose her place in the book of

The Silver Trumpet                    79

calculations she is always reading, but the trumpet seems to have some kind of spiritual quality and instead of being angry at the interruption she is transported back to a memory of when she and her sister were babies, before they grew so different from one another. She even wonders if perhaps she is not quite so much wiser than her sister than she generally assumes herself to be. The sound of the silver trumpet has a great harmonising and pacifying effect throughout the castle as a whole, upon the staff and their inter-relationships. However, when the trumpet call ends, all goes back to as it was before.

The young prince introduces himself to the king as Prince Courtesy, and says he is in search of adventures and also seeks a maiden to be his future queen. The king can promise no adventures but says he has two daughters, either of which the prince can have as long as he first wins her heart.

The prince is then left in the company of a strange dwarf, who appears to fulfil the role of court jester, mostly by the performance of grotesque dances. He is an enigmatic although apparently wise and good figure, despite his strange actions and appearance. His rapid mode of speech and use of long and strange words make it difficult for the prince to understand what he says but the young man feels *in his bones* that the little creature means to be good and kindly to him. This phrase is not only italicised in the book but is repeated in full capitals. HE FELT IT IN HIS BONES.

This suggests a clue is being provided to the discerning reader as to the nature of the dwarf, who is known to the court as the Little Fat Podger. In the course of the story he becomes the agent for both good and ill events and in the context of Barfield's anthroposophical thought might well be a representation of the physical world, that ground which provides the pabulum for representations we make of it with the cognitive imagination. Such speculation is somewhat out of the intellectual realm of the nursery, but is nonetheless worthy of reflection in light of Barfield's later works for an adult and intellectually sophisticated audience.

The dwarf finds the prince's attitude of actually *looking* for adventures to be very questionable, but leads him to the garden where the two princesses are to be found, with the advice, given in song accompanied by a grotesque sideways dance, to: "Take Violetta. Much better, much better, if you can get her, without Gambetta." It seems rather odd, and unexplained, that he should revert to their original names at this point, whereas in the story the two girls continue to be referred to by their later names of Violet and Gamboy.

The prince at first finds himself in some confusion as he comes upon Gamboy sitting by herself and is rudely snubbed by her. Then he meets Violet, and thinking it to be the same girl, is puzzled as to why her attitude seems to have changed so abruptly when she receives him kindly. The misunderstanding is soon sorted out as he recalls the dwarf's advice that the two girls are identical in appearance. From then on friendship burgeons between the prince and Violet, and he is easily able to tell them apart. Violet continues to love her sister, even more than the prince at first, although the prince does not care at all for Gamboy, who he feels is always intruding upon their happiness.

One day the prince brings some musicians to the garden. They are five in number and produce wondrous harmonies that have an effect similar to the prince's original silver trumpet call. As the music plays it appears to the two girls like bands of colour intertwining in beautiful patterns. In the silence afterwards all three wander around the garden, arm in arm, east of the sun as it sets, and west of the moon as it rises, in an atmosphere of such calm that even Gamboy has no cross word to utter, and the memory of the evening remains as a soothing image even in far later days.

The Little Fat Podger explains the reason for this to the prince. Music hath charms, he says, and he evokes the terms harmony, form and chaos, light and darkness, and the power of the dominant seventh. All this is rather over the prince's head, who simply seeks practical advice on how to keep Gamboy in a gentle mood. "What about your silver trumpet, you nin-a-kin?" retorts the dwarf.

Accordingly, when Gamboy reverts to her usual abrasive behaviour, the prince takes up his trumpet and blows it once more. It reduces her to a dreaming state which makes things more pleasant for the prince and Violet but unfortunately it does not last. The prince has to keep playing the silver trumpet, and although it has the desired effect for a time, when Gamboy wakes up she only seems doubly virulent, as if to make up for the time she was peacefully asleep.

Eventually the prince asks Violet to marry him, and although she is sure that she wants to, she feels that she ought to ask someone else's advice before committing herself. She goes looking for her sister but meets the dwarf first. He shouts hooray and says that her answer must be yes, but warns her not to tell Gamboy about it. Violet insists that she ought to tell her, whereupon the dwarf, who hates Gamboy as much as he loves Violet, concedes her point but, wise to Gamboy's ways, tells her to listen very carefully to what she might say.

Violet goes to Gamboy, who as usual is casting up accounts, but when Violet tells her the news, Gamboy cries that she hates the prince and that if Violet marries him she will have nothing more to do with her, so which of the two of them is she going to choose? At this stark confrontation something snaps in Violet's mind. Her love for the prince is strong enough to break the spell cast by Miss Thomson and henceforth she loves the prince most of all in all the world, and her sister only second. Then off Violet goes to the prince to tell him she is happy to marry him straight away.

Until the wedding the prince and Violet remain happy in each other's company in spite of Gamboy constantly and deliberately getting in their way. This distresses Violet for she still loves Gamboy, but as Barfield points out to his young readers, there are two ways of loving people. Violet's way is to like seeing them well and happy; and Gamboy's way is to like them to do what you tell them.

For his part the prince is somewhat worried that he might marry the wrong one by mistake on the day, but the dwarf reminds him that upon their 21st birthday they will no longer have to dress identically, according to the rules of the kingdom, and from thenceforth can wear what they like. Thus he delays the wedding until their coming of age. When this occurs, their internal difference is now outwardly marked by their outer show of self-expression in their clothes. Gamboy prefers black, straight, narrow dresses, with her hair scraped back into a bun. Violet appears in white billowing dresses with her hair piled high on her head set off with a silver comb.

At the marriage, the old king decides to abdicate so that henceforth the prince becomes King Courtesy, and with Queen Violet rules the land, while Gamboy grows ever more spiteful and jealous.

At this point events in the story suggest a heavy subtext of hidden meanings.

The silver trumpet is lost on the wedding night. Although the prince has been warned in the past never to part with it, Violet chafes him into giving it to her, which he does. Put to one side, no doubt because the couple are more concerned with each other upon their wedding night, the silver trumpet is discovered by Gamboy who promptly hides it.

Coincident with the loss of the silver trumpet, the harvest in the kingdom that year is so bad and that the people are starving and even on the point of revolt, stirred up by a mysterious woman agitator. As one might suspect, this turns out to be Gamboy in disguise, an art at which she is apparently highly skilled.

At the end of this disastrous year Violet gives birth to a baby daughter, but remains at the point of death herself. This fact the king tries to conceal from the populace, for fear that he will be blamed for the situation, by keeping all the palace lights blazing, which only serves to incite rather than to pacify the hungry citizens, who strangely know nothing of Violet's pregnancy.

Even more strangely the Little Fat Podger, despite being a member of the court, does not know of it either. This leads to his being manipulated by Gamboy into a wicked scheme which has profound and lasting consequences.

In his role as court jester he has been hard put to keep King Courtesy cheerful amid all his problems but one day he finds him in the garden laughing at the antics of a great clumsy green toad. The Podger, who specialises in making contraptions into which he clambers and cavorts in order to amuse people (a favourite speciality being a grass hopper) hastens to produce a model of a great toad.

Gamboy sees him trying out this toad model and on the spur of the moment conceives a cruel plan. She asks him to take a note immediately to Violet's room. The dwarf, who knows nothing of the queen's pregnancy and the need to keep her quiet in her weakened condition, goes up to her room in his grotesque toad-like form. Violet takes one look at this hideous appearance dancing about her room, screams and dies of fright.

Not realising what has happened because of the encumbrance of his device, in which he can hear nothing of her screams, the dwarf keeps dancing grotesquely before the terrified baby, until the illuminated eyes of the monstrous form light up the dead form of his mistress. In this odd detail within the story there seems to be a resonance with one of the conditions of human consciousness that is illustrated at the end of Barfield's book, published some forty years later, *Worlds Apart.* Here he conjures an allegorical image of a man with a head like a round box with two holes in it, in which there is a source of light which blazes out of the eye holes. This he describes as a stage of human conscious evolution called Subjective Idealism, preliminary to two further stages that he calls the Key to the Kingdom, and the Kingdom.

Whatever we like to make of this parallel, there is an ambience of death about this whole scenario that is reminiscent of parts of *The Chemical Marriage of Christian Rosencreutz,* which is essentially, in the midst of all its baroque symbolism, a death and resurrection story. Immediately upon Queen Violet's death, King Courtesy, despite his youth, becomes like a decrepit old man.

Their child lives however, and is christened Lily, whether or not in conscious emulation of Goethe's *Green Snake and the Beautiful Lily* is another matter for conjecture. The dwarf, held responsible for her mother's death, is taken off to prison and is said to have died in jail, talking continually of his dreadful mistake until he quietly passes away.

It appears as if Lily is going to take the place of her mother in her father's affections. They become close companions even before she is a year old, and in time is found to be a beautiful natural dancer, without having to be taught a single step. With the companionship of his daughter as she grows older, the king gradually becomes able to resume his royal duties, the harvests are abundant and all unrest in the populace becomes a thing of the past.

There is an intimate polarity in the relationship between King Courtesy and Princess Lily. He reads to her from ancient tales and she dances for him, making her own dresses appropriate for them. The dances she improvises follow the seasons of Spring, Summer, Autumn and Winter. The Autumn one she calls her Leaf Dance, but it so reminds the king of Queen Violet, who used to dance like a leaf in the wind, that to avoid making him sad again in this way Lily does not repeat that particular dance.

Meanwhile Gamboy, now generally referred to as Aunt Gamboy, is busy in the background. She has no time for dancing, and only appears from time to time to sneer at the activity. Her principal social activity is to host meetings of what are known as the Amalgamated Princesses, who seem to represent much that Barfield did not care for in the modern world, insofar that they seem to be entertained at receptions where aerated bread and desiccated coconut are the main delicacies. Gamboy's constant reading is a black bound book called *Excerpta* which seems to be some kind of potted encyclopaedia of dubious knowledge of a quasi-scientific kind.

So things continue until Lily is about seven to eight years old, (life periods in periods of seven are quite important to Steiner's educational and psychological theory, it might be said), and then Aunt Gamboy's attitude begins slowly to change. She is less sharp with the king, indeed almost kind, perhaps having noticed his loneliness for, despite the presence of Lily, he seems to miss her mother more and more as the child grows, and no doubt Gamboy notices this.

One autumn afternoon a strange thing happens. The king is out with Lily on a country walk when suddenly the child screams and faints. They have come upon a toad, and whilst it makes the king laugh, as on a notable occasion before, it terrifies Lily on account of the circumstances of her mother's death, when the dwarf had appeared as a capering toad with illuminated eyes. The king assures his daughter that there is nothing to be frightened of in any of God's creatures, but all to no avail.

When Aunt Gamboy is appraised of the incident she says that of course Lily must be taught to conquer her silly fear, that she will from henceforth take particular care of her, and let her sleep next to her room. But in fact she sets about making Lily even more frightened, with subtly introduced suggestions of horror of the unknown, so that the child becomes frightened of almost everything. She cannot even bring herself to mention the word "toad". At the same time Gamboy advises her not to confide in her father, for men do not understand these things.

Gamboy begins deliberately to increase her domination over Lily's father in subtle ways, to the point that he feels ever more grateful to her and even to identify her with his long lost Queen Violet. Lily also begins to look upon Gamboy as her own mother, although it is cold comfort she gets from her in response to her nightmares of being chased by a toad from which her father cannot protect her, as he has become no more than a diminutive giggling figure.

We have thus reached a new stage in the story, where death has given place to degradation and the rising in power of Aunt Gamboy.

A new character now appears in the form of Prince Peerio. He has been banished by his father from his own kingdom for declining to marry the rich heiress that has been found for him. The reason for this is that he possesses a portrait of Princess

Lily that has come his way at the hands of a wandering merchant and on the strength of this has fallen in love with her and is determined to find her.

He has set off on foot on his quest to find the original of this picture and walked so far that he completes a circuit of the whole earth, and is puzzled to find himself back in the same place again. Baffled by this experience he seeks room at an inn, but all rooms being taken, he is accepted on the staff as a kitchen hand. He serves at table and also gets to know a strange little cook who instructs him in "cosmic circumambulation" by means of flattening out an orange peel by way of demonstration.

In short, Mountainy Castle, which is the home of Princess Lily, is plainly a place that is not gained by following terrestrial directions. This accords with another anthroposophical insight about cosmic and terrestrial directions. To go to the desired other world, be it the Isles of the Blessed, or Avalon or Eldorado, it is necessary to travel in a cosmic direction not a terrestrial one. Much the same conceit appears in Tolkien regarding the lands of the Valar. To travel terrestrially in any particular direction simply results in going round in an earthbound circle.

The hint is elaborated when Peerio sees an image of himself in the spherical surface of a polished serving dish and laughs at the porky appearance of himself therein. This is a hint as to why the Little Fat Podger looks as he does, for he appears to be closely associated with physical worldly appearances or modes of being.

As he says to Peerio after his instruction in cosmic directions, people who live in glass houses should not throw stones. We, as spiritual beings, are all in the same terrestrial boat, seeing ourselves as distorted reflections within the world of the terrestrial sphere. So when the cook asks Peerio why he walked around the world, and Peerio tells him, the cook responds by singing the first line of a song, "Let the great big world keep tur... ", and there stops. The hint being that to meet the desired objective one does not complete the turning.

The cook now asks to see the picture that Peerio possesses and recognises it as Princess Lily, for as by now we may have guessed, the cook turns out to be the Little Fat Podger. He did not after all die in prison, but was allowed "to pass quietly away" into exile by those who suspected the true story behind his predicament. He provides Peerio with a letter of introduction to Miss Thomson, whose help he judges will be essential when trying to deal with the machinations of someone like Aunt Gamboy.

On his arrival at Mountainy, Prince Peerio meets with a stable boy who tells him how things are in the kingdom. Things have apparently been going from bad to worse. There seems to be a spell on the place and everyone walks round with glum expressions and hushed voices, whilst Gamboy, whose movements are also as silent as a spider or an ant, seems to rule the roost. The King stays shut up in his room all day staring at the wall and seems to think that Gamboy is his queen, whilst the Amalgamated Princesses are frequent visitors who act as if the place belonged to them.

In fact the Amalgamated Princesses appear so often because they have to pay subscriptions to Gamboy who, in return, offers them advice on how to destabilise the kingdoms they come from. Whilst they accept this advice with overweening ambition, they do not realise that it is not in their own interest that they are receiving this dearly bought advice, but that when they have destabilised their own kingdoms Gamboy will seize the opportunity to have the troops of her own kingdom march in to take them all over. Gamboy appears to have much of the modern world about her.

Princess Lily remains shut up in a high tower, weak and irritable, almost unrecognisable from her former self, no longer being read to by the king, no longer dancing, terrified of everything, of her own shadow, of darkness, of banging doors, her bedroom windows fast shut in case a toad tries to enter in the night.

Unknown to the two boys, Queen Gamboy, as she now styles herself, can hear all they say by her magic arts. From a high window she reads out a spell from her great black book as Peerio stands dreaming of Lily in the grounds below, and suddenly the unfortunate youth finds himself transformed into a toad. Fortunately, however, he still retains the letter of introduction to Miss Thomson.

Meanwhile, the stable boy has gone off to resume his duties and by some whim decides to climb up into the loft to take a nap. Here, to his surprise, he finds in the hay the long lost silver trumpet. He takes it up and blows it.

The results of this spiritual clarion call in the enchanted land are quite remarkable. While the trumpet is playing the spell lifts from the castle, people look round and stare at each other in surprise, but then relapse back to their old ways when the trumpet call ends. The boy blows it again, and this time is has the effect of awakening Lily to the extent of being able to send off a message to Miss Thomson at her home in Bee Cottage. What seems even more remarkable is that it even causes the dead Queen Violet to stir in her grave.

The king is also sufficiently revived to send for whoever sounded the trumpet, and it is restored to him, and the stable boy tells the citizens all that has happened.

Lily's messenger reaches Miss Thomson who affirms that she is always ready to help anyone who has the courage to ask her.

She makes off for the castle, meeting Prince Peerio, in his form as a toad, on the way. She reads the letter of introduction he clasps but to his consternation tells him that she is unable herself to turn him back into his princely shape. That can only be done by someone who loves him in his present form. Peerio finds this somewhat depressing news but she gives him some advice on how best to go about it.

She then proceeds to the tower and asks Princess Lily why she is so miserable and frightened, eliciting from her her fear of toads. Upon this admission Miss Thomson asks why she should ever be frightened of one of God's creatures, which reminds Lily that her father had told her much the same thing. You only have to get to know them, Miss Thomson continues, and you will not do that by shutting yourself up in a tower. In any case, being afraid of something is not a reason for running away from it.

She reminds Lily of the stories that her father used to read to her and asks if she does not want to be like the princesses she heard about then. This reminds Lily of brave heroines like Alcestis and Imogen, and as she sits thinking about them.

There is a transformation element in the Greek myth of Alcestis wherein her husband Admetus neglected to make the customary marriage sacrifice whereupon, when he entered the bridal chamber, he was met not by his bride but a knot of hissing vipers. However, Barfield probably has in mind the story of how Alcestis was later remarkable for having such love for her husband that she volunteered to die in his stead when his destined day of death arrived. Brave Imogen is a leading character in the immense complexities of Shakespeare's *Cymbeline.*

Miss Thomson, taking Lily's thoughful silence for consent, returns home. On the way she passes the ditch in which the toad is sitting, and simply says: "Tonight!"

That night, Lily plucks up the courage to sleep alone, without guards or servants at hand, and with her window open wide. As she lies in the dark her fear becomes almost unbearable, particularly when she hears something flop through the window. Prince Peerio realises her terror as she confronts him in his toad form, but in spite of this she knows what she must do, and kisses him on his icy head. Immediately, the moon comes out from behind the clouds and she sees before her, not a toad, but a handsome prince, complete in silver chain mail.

The prince is as surprised as she to find himself in this shining mail for he had left it at home when he started on his wanderings, but Miss Thomson had fashioned it for him out of dreams, and put it on him when he himself in his human form was but a dream and the toad was the walking reality. An interesting conception this, on Barfield's part, that concurs with Steiner's teaching on different planes of consciousness.

As might be expected, Prince Peerio marries Princess Lily. Her father, King Courtesy, is brought down from his room in a litter to witness it, as is Queen Gamboy, released from jail for the occasion, after having received a severe drubbing from the young prince before her confinement to prison. When they go to take her back to jail after the ceremony he stops them, and taking the silver trumpet, sounds a series of clarion calls. As he does so, Gamboy's features begin to soften and to change, until to the astonishment and delight of all, they see it is Queen Violet who is standing before them.

Her first action is to ask for the silver trumpet. When it is given to her she turns and hands it to her husband, King Courtesy. There is a slight inconsistency here for according to the story he has already received it from the stable boy. However, upon receiving it back from she to whom he gave it in the first place, he also is transformed. His back straightens, and at the behest of Queen Violet, he vows never to release it from his keeping again and to guard it in future even with his life.

There are some who say that at this time a certain corpse in the likeness of Queen Violet began to turn into that of Queen Gamboy, but others dispute the tale. In any case, in the course of time the neglected grave is forgotten and crumbles to ruin, and some even doubt that the whole thing ever existed.

The older couple, King Courtesy and Queen Violet, now voluntarily make way for the rule of King Peerio and Queen Lily, the five musicians reappear together with Miss Thomson and the Little Fat Podger and all ends with great merriment in a dance upon the green. Thus the tale ends in appropriate fairy tale fashion.

To judge from extant letters, *The Silver Trumpet* served very well indeed as a children's story and, whether intended or not, seems to be have been influenced very much by imaginations induced by the teachings of Rudolf Steiner. Although conversely, it will be found that it is a characteristic of many fairy stories, whether from Perrault, the Brothers Grimm, or Hans Christian Anderson, to have characteristics that link them to the romantic neo-platonic tradition.

# XIII

## ANNOTATED BIBLIOGRAPHY

A proportion of Barfield's published work is in the form of collected essays and lecture scripts and so with this short annotated select bibliography we provide a brief guide for those who wish to encounter Barfield's intense and thought provoking intellectual challenges directly.

The titles against which an asterisk has been placed indicate those works that have already been dealt with in the main text. These represent Barfield's more literary and imaginative works where we feel that our specialist insights may have been able to contribute a fresh and individual viewpoint. It is beyond our competence and the scope of this book to make a critical evaluation of his more directly philosophical works.

A work that may prove a helpful intermediate step for students is *A Barfield Reader*, edited by G.B.Tennyson (Wesleyan University Press 1999) which besides an Introduction by the Editor contains extracts from *Poetic Diction, History in English Words, The Rediscovery of Meaning, Saving the Appearances, History, Guilt & Habit, Romanticism Comes of Age, The Case for Anthroposophy, The Silver Trumpet, Orpheus, This Ever Diverse Pair, Worlds Apart* and *Unancestral Voice,* together with three poems.

A festschrift produced in celebration of Barfield's 75th birthday, entitled *Evolution of Consciousness, Studies in Polarity,* edited by Shirley Sugerman (Wesleyan University Press 1976), is also of interest, not least for containing a comprehensive Barfield bibliography.

## The Silver Trumpet [1925] *

Described and reviewed in main text.

## History In English Words [1926]

A brief consecutive history of the peoples who have spoken the derivatives of the Indo-European tongue, illustrated at all points by current English words whose derivation, history of use and changes of meaning record and unlock the larger history of those who spoke them. How in the language the past history of humanity is spread out like a map, just as the history of the mineral earth lies embedded in the layers of its outer crust, demonstrating that language has preserved for us the inner history of man's soul through the evolution of human consciousness.

## Poetic Diction [1928]

Subtitled, *a Study in Meaning*. It aims to present not merely a theory of poetic diction but a theory of poetry and a theory of knowledge. Only by imagination can the world be known, so what is needed is not larger and larger telescopes or more and more powerful microscopes but that the human mind should become increasingly aware of its own creative activity. Particularly as, outside poetry and the arts, this creativity proceeds at an unconscious level, where perception is the point where life and the imagination meet.

The study of poetry is valuable for other purposes than the better enjoyment of poetry; it can be a way to prove the existence of an inner world by personal experience. The book attempts to show how this can be achieved by reflection on the poetic use of language.

### *Romanticism Comes Of Age [1944]*

A collection of essays that, apart from any wider significance they may possess, affords the best demonstration of the paramount debt that Owen Barfield owes to Rudolf Steiner. They extend over a long period and were contributed to periodicals published by or associated with the Anthroposophical Society. The actual essays vary slightly in different editions but all date from before 1944 in the first edition, and 1949 in the expanded later editions.

Essay titles are: *From East to West; Thinking and Thought; Speech, Reason and Imagination; Of the Consciousness Soul; The Form of Hamlet; Of the Intellectual Soul; The Philosophy of Samuel Taylor Coleridge; Goethe and the Twentieth Century; The Time-Philosophy of Rudolf Steiner; The Fall in Man and Nature; Man, Thought and Nature; Rudolf Steiner's Concept of Mind.*

It presents the history of the last few centuries in terms of Steiner's notion that consciousness has been evolving through a necessary but rather bleak stage in order to develop individuality, the thesis being illustrated by references to Shakespeare, Coleridge and Goethe, thus providing a demonstration of how Romanticism is coming of age.

### *This Ever Diverse Pair [1950]* *

Described and reviewed in main text.

### *Saving The Appearances [1957]*

The greater part of this important book consists of an attempt to focus on the gulf that exists between the atomic physical structure of matter and the appearances of the familiar world, a gulf which is usually ignored. This involves challenging the common assumption that, from the ancient world to modern times, there is a constant unchanging psychological interconnection between man and the world about him. Barfield shows that this assumption is an illusion that arose in the first place through clearly traceable historical causes.

The result is a book that forms an outline sketch of the history of human consciousness, particularly that of western humanity, over the last 3000 years or so. Once we abandon the above illusory assumption the consequences are very far reaching, concerned with new insights into the origin, the current predicament and the future destiny of man.

### Worlds Apart [1963]  *

Described and reviewed in main text.

### Unancestral Voice  [1965]  *

Described and reviewed in main text.

### Speaker's Meaning  [1967]  *

Described and reviewed in main text.

### What Coleridge Thought  [1971]

An important contribution to Coleridge studies, dedicated to the leading Coleridge scholar and editor of his letters, notebooks and marginalia, Kathleen Coburn, "with admiration, gratitude and affection".

Written to try to provide what another distinguished Coleridge scholar, Professor J.A.Appleyard, wrote in the Introduction of his own *Coleridge's Philosophy of Literature:* "What is wanting in the sizeable bibliography of literature on Coleridge is a full-scale study of the development of his philosophy which will consider him on his own terms and not as a representative of something else, whether it be German idealism, English Platonism, pantheistic mysticism, semantic analysis, or depth psychology. The idea or organising insight ought to be internal to his thought, so as to see what that thought is and not merely what it is like or unlike."

Most students picking up a contemporary book on Coleridge in order to find out what he thought about things, are likely to find themselves involved in a complex and allusive web of comparative philosophy, which is not what most of them need at all, for it keeps them outside the intellectual content of Coleridge's mind. It hinders people from reading Coleridge in the only way he wanted to be read, for his object was not to indoctrinate but to goad his readers into thinking for themselves - "to excite the germinal power that craves no knowledge but what it can take up into itself."

Barfield assists the modern reader toward this by recourse to Coleridge's scattered writings, most of which, apart from *Biographia Literaria* and *Lectures on Shakespeare* are not easily available, and which were never systematically developed into a single work, but distributed piecemeal in a mass of note books, marginalia, anecdotes of friends and acquaintances, lecture notes, some patchy prose works and a few gems of poetry. Here will be found the heart of Coleridge's thinking, with chapters on *Thoughts and Thinking, Naturata and Naturans, Two Forces of One Power; Life; Outness; Imagination and Fancy; Understanding; Reason; Ideas, Methods and Laws; Coleridge and the Cosmology of Science, Man and God;* and *Man in History and in Society.*

### The Rediscovery Of Meaning [1977]

A number of lectures and essays on widely different topics over a period from 1946 to 1976, although with the bulk of them after 1960. It is divided into two parts.

The first, entitled *Meaning, Language and Imagination* contains *The Rediscovery of Meaning; Dream, Myth and Philosophical Double Vision; The Meaning of "Literal"; Poetic Diction and Legal Fiction; The Harp and the Camera; Where is Fancy Bred? The Rediscovery of Allegory; Imagination and Inspiration; Language and Discovery.*

The second part, entitled *Man, Society and God* comprises *Matter, Imagination and Spirit; Self and Reality; Science and Quality; The Coming Trauma of Materialism; Participation and Isolation – a Fresh Light on Present Discontents; Form and Art in Society; Philology and the Incarnation; The Psalms of David; The "Son of God" and the "Son of Man".*

### History, Guilt And Habit [1979]

Three lectures that, although capable of standing on their own, and delivered to different audiences, have also what Owen Barfield hoped would be recognised as a fundamental "tri-unity".

*History of Ideas: Evolution of Consciousness* is in effect a résumé of Barfield's first full length works, *History in English Words* with its insight that the history of language contains a record of the evolution of human consciousness, and *Poetic Diction* where his distinction between perception and thinking, grounded in Romantic and Coleridgean philosophy, forms the framework for an examination of the language of poetry. He also draws the distinction between the evolution of consciousness and the history of ideas, which are frequently in danger of being confused or conflated.

*Modern Idolatry: the Sin of Literalness* revisits the key concepts of his important book *Saving the Appearances,* making it plain that the use of the term "idolatry" is no mere fanciful use of a theological concept but an accurate description of the actual state of received modern consciousness. Applying the concepts of polarity and the evolution of consciousness he demonstrates how the modern perception of the world is dangerously one-sided and at root the chief cause of modern alienation, sin, madness and the modern problem of guilt.

*The Force of Habit* looks toward the future with a view to what should be done in the face of the unbalance in our received thinking-perceiving to free ourselves from the tyranny of habitually looking at the outside instead of the inside of things. His proposed personal reformation for each one of us is a prescription that resonates with his more imaginative works *This Ever Diverse Pair, Worlds Apart* and *Unancestral Voice.*

### *Orpheus [1983]* *

Described and reviewed in main text.

# INDEX

## About this Series:

"The Magical Worlds" series, of which this is the third volume, focuses on the works of renowned literary figures. The first four volumes deal with the group known as "The Inklings." This coterie of influential authors consisted of J.R.R.Tolkien, C.S.Lewis, Owen Barfield, and Charles Williams. Each volume examines one of these authors from the viewpoint of Knight's valuable experience and insight into the realm of the creative imagination and its relationship to the magical powers of the human soul.

Owen Barfield, writing of the manuscript from which these volumes developed, had this to say: *"Because of the combination of information, understanding and insight on which it is founded, [the work] is more than outstanding. It is not in the same league with anything else I have come across."*